Walter Francis Willcox

Area and Population of the United States at the Eleventh

Census

Walter Francis Willcox

Area and Population of the United States at the Eleventh Census

ISBN/EAN: 9783337405250

Printed in Europe, USA, Canada, Australia, Japan

Cover: Foto ©Suzi / pixelio.de

More available books at **www.hansebooks.com**

AMERICAN ECONOMIC ASSOCIATION

ECONOMIC STUDIES

VOL. II.   No. 4.

PUBLISHED BI-MONTHLY
PRICE, $2.50 PER YEAR

AREA AND POPULATION OF THE UNITED STATES AT THE ELEVENTH CENSUS

BY

WALTER F. WILLCOX, Ph.D.

AUGUST, 1897

PUBLISHED FOR THE
AMERICAN ECONOMIC ASSOCIATION
BY THE MACMILLAN COMPANY
NEW YORK
LONDON : SWAN SONNENSCHEIN & CO.

AREA AND POPULATION OF THE UNITED STATES
AT THE ELEVENTH CENSUS

PREFACE.

This Study is the first part of a projected Introduction to the Social Statistics of the United States. It will be followed shortly by another on the Density and Distribution of their population. From this standpoint the prefatory chapter should be judged. Both Studies are the outcome of lectures on Social Statistics offered to university undergraduates and are published primarily for their convenience, but may be suggestive to others engaged in teaching or studying the subject. The writer's conception of statistics is that it is a method of giving precision to knowledge by making quantitative and verifiable statements possible in some fields where they have been precluded. The comparative insignificance for social science of the topics which the statistical method frees from the subjectivity of personal opinion or individual observation should not blind one to the important fact that this method contributes to make progress in knowledge possible by liberating certain aspects of it from the labyrinth of personal and unverifiable argument.

WALTER F. WILLCOX.

Cornell university,
July, 1897.

CONTENTS.

LIST OF TABLES.

INTRODUCTION TO SOCIAL STATISTICS.

The meaning of the word statistics is still a subject of some dispute. In such a case the ultimate authority is not its etymology, but current usage. This authority is often vague in its utterances, and offers only an uncertain or ambiguous meaning which persons wishing to employ the word with scientific precision, may make more exact, though they may not overrule usage. Judged by this standard, the word statistics refers to the direct or indirect results of counting in the real world about the observer, and no further definite content can be assigned it. The counting may have occurred in any portion of the world. The estimate of the number of stars from enumeration of those in a certain field and multiplication results in statistics. The figures expressing the annual production of iron, lumber or beef, or the average daily attendance at a fair are statistics. Whenever the word is used, the thought is suspended until the subject to which the figures refer is made known. Statistics of *a*, *b*, or *c* is always the rounded notion. Nor is this an error of popular speech, which is avoided by exact writers, for experts give it the same meaning. During the meetings of the International Statistical Institute at Chicago in 1893, papers were offered upon agriculture, railways, education, anthropometry, marriage and divorce and crime, and they were all welcomed as statistical.[1] By the concurrence of popular and scientific usage, then, the word statistics refers to the results obtained in any field of reality by methods of counting.[2]

[1] Bulletin de L'Institut International de Statistique, Tome VIII, Première Livraison. 1895.

[2] Rümelin, Reden und Aufsätze, 1875, p. 226.

The word statistics is derived from the same source as state, but the latter has two root meanings, a condition, as the state of one's health, and a political body, as the state of Portugal, and from which of the two statistics is a branch has been disputed.[1] Probably, however, statistics is derived from state in the sense of a political body and the word then means etymologically the science of states. Its history in brief, is as follows :[2]

Early in the sixteenth century, and partly under the influence of Machiavelli,[3] the disinterested study of politics revived. Its practical aspects received in Italian the name of *ragione di stato*, or in barbarous Latin the equivalent *ratio status*. In these phrases *stato* or *status* was the generic name for a political body, while the older and more usual terms, *res publica*, *civitas* and *imperium*, were restricted to specific kinds of political bodies. From *stato* in this sense was formed the Italian *statista*, the German and English *statist*, a statesman,[4]

[1] Some have claimed that both meanings of state were implicate in statistics. This notion apparently finds expression in the definition of Webster, "a collection of facts respecting the condition of the people in a state."

[2] V. John, Der Name Statistik, in Zeitschrift für Schweizerische Statistik, 1883 ; Eng. trans. in J. Royal Stat. Soc., 46 : 656-679, (1883). V. John, Geschichte der Statistik, pp. 4-11. A. Gabaglio, Teoria Generale della Statistica, Vol. 1, p. 59, Vol. 2, p. 1.

[3] "We find in him for the first time since Aristotle the pure passionless curiosity of the man of science."—Pollock, History of the Science of Politics, p. 42.

[4] Examples of the early use of statist in English, with the meaning of statesman are :
1602 : I once did hold it, as our statists do,
      A baseness to write fair and laboured much
      How to forget that learning . . . Shakspere, Hamlet, 5 : 2 : 33.

and from this the adjective *statisticus*, relating to a statesman. The new studies in practical political science were called *disciplina politico-statistica* or in abbreviated form, *statistics*. That word thus became the name for the studies deemed of especial value to one aspiring to enter the service of a state.

The difference between the present and the original meaning of statist and statistics is explained by the fact that the latter word was adopted nearly a century ago as the name of a study having a distinct origin, and previously called " political arithmetic." This study of society by the enumerating method had its origin in England, and its inspiration in the triumphs of mathematical and inductive methods gained in other fields by members of the embryonic Royal Society. It began

1609 :   I do believe
              (Statist though I am none nor like to be)
              That this will prove a war.—Shakspere, Cymbeline, 2 : 4 : 16.
1654 : (*written much earlier*) To you the statists of long-flourishing
              Rome.—Webster, Appius and Virginia, 1 : 4
1643 : Among statists and lawyers.—Milton, Doctrine and Discipline of Divorce.
1671 : Statists indeed and lovers of their country.—Milton, Paradise
              Regained, 4 : 354.
As statist in this sense is obsolete the attempt to revive the word as a brief and euphonious substitute for statistician seems to deserve encouragement. A few illustrations of this use may be given.
1870 : The keen statist reckons by tens and hundreds.—Emerson,
              Society and Solitude, (ed. 1876), p. 270.
1877 : The high rate of infant mortality continues to occupy the
              earnest attention of medical statists.—Farr, Vital Statistics, p. 190.
1895 : How pleased I am to meet again such a body of statists. I
              like the old and short word.—W. W. Folwell, in Proceedings of Nat. Ass'n of Officials of Bureaus of Labor Statistics,
              p. 54.

with Captain John Graunt, who published his Natural and Political Observations in 1662.[1] His conclusions were mainly social rather than physical or biological, and the same is still true of the results obtained by the statistical method. There is, therefore, justification for giving political arithmetic the shorter name derived from the organized political life of man. Popular instinct and language were not entirely at fault. While the enumerating method has never been confined to the study of governmental phenomena, yet it is mainly used for the investigation of some aspect of man's social life. This fact is loosely expressed in both terms, political arithmetic and statistics.

As the applications of the statistical method widen, it seems better to add some modifying word or phrase defining the subject. The work of which this Study is the opening part will be concerned with the applications of the statistical method to man's social life ; it is therefore entitled Social Statistics. The primary aim, to interest students of society in an unfamiliar method, may be furthered by showing it at work and in connection with its results better than by mere discussion of method. Statements of fact have been incorporated not primarily for their own sake but to elucidate the method. Only the simplest topics under the simplest division, viz., demography or the statistics of population, will be treated, because they best reveal and illustrate it, and in nearly every instance the illustrative facts will be drawn from some portion of the United States.

[1] Natural and Political Observations mentioned in a following Index and made upon the Bills of Mortality by John Graunt, Citizen of London. London, 1662.

CHAPTER I.

AREA OF THE UNITED STATES AND ITS DIVISIONS.

Area is usually treated in books on statistics as an unquestionable datum, but the imperfect condition of American surveys makes a brief criticism necessary. Otherwise the trustworthiness of subsequent determinations of the ratio between area and population, *i. e.*, density of population, would be matter of faith rather than of reason. By area is meant the number of units of surface included within certain boundaries, on the assumption that the included surface is all at the level of the sea. In determinations of area the unit of reference is a square degree. Since its area varies with its distance from the equator, the area for each degree of latitude, and so that between the equator and any two adjacent meridians may be requisite as units. From the measurements of a standard authority on the subject[1] the area of the earth's surface, land and water together, is computed as 509,950,778 square kilometers or about 196,899,795 square miles.

The area of any country is the sum of all the square degrees lying entirely within its bounds, and of such parts of the degrees cut by the boundary as lie within the country. The former are found from Bessel's tables or by a geodetic formula; the latter are measured by

[1] F. W. Bessel and J. J. Bäyer, Gradmessung in Ostpreussen, Berlin, 1838. Compare M. Levasseur in B. de L'Inst. Int. de Statistique, 1886, 2ème Livraison, p. 23.

the polar planimeter on accurate maps. The maps of the United States, the theme of this Study, are of varying excellence and no accurate maps of the boundary of Alaska exist. Hence the official statement of its area " may easily be ten per cent. in error."[1] The boundary of the United States between the Lake of the Woods, Minnesota, and lake Superior, and between Schoodic lake, Maine, and the Atlantic ocean is also imperfectly mapped, but the possible error resulting from the uncertain location of these two fragments of our boundary is very slight. The standard measurement of the area of the United States was made by Mr. Henry Gannett and Mr. F. DeY. Carpenter in connection with the Tenth Census.[2] In defining the boundaries of the country, they excluded the sea within the three mile limit and the portions of the Great Lakes subject to the jurisdiction of the United States, but could state no rule with regard to the treatment of bays or gulfs. While Long Island sound was excluded, Delaware and Chesapeake bays were not. The area of the United States, within the limits thus defined, was measured as 3,025,600 square miles. To this should be added 531,000 square miles as the official estimate of the area of Alaska[3] and an undetermined amount as this country's share of the Great Lakes. The latter is estimated by M. Levasseur[4] as 133,000 square kilometers or about 51,350 square miles, and the total area of the United States excluding the sea within the

[1] Mr. Henry Gannett in a personal letter to the author.

[2] Tenth Census, Bulletin, The Areas of the United States, Washington, 1881.

[3] Eleventh Census, Alaska, p. 11.

[4] Op. cit., 2ème Livraison, 1887, p. 204.

three mile limit would thus be about 3,607,950 square miles.

Light is thrown upon the territorial position of the United States by a comparison with that of other great powers. The land surface of the globe is stated by various authorities as follows:

| AUTHORITY. | Date. | Land surface in | | Per cent. of total earth's surface. |
		square kilometers.	square miles.	
Levasseur[1]	1886	136,100,000	52,160,000	26.5
Ravenstein[2]	1890		51,250,800	26.0
Wagner and Supan[3] .	1891	135,490,765	52,330 000	26.6
Juraschek[4]	1893	135,454,265	52,300,000	26.6

Probably between twenty-six and twenty-seven per cent. of the earth's surface is land. As inland water surfaces are treated differently by different authorities, the divergencies shown in the table may be due in part to differences in definition of land surface and certainly are due in part to differences of measurement.

A few great powers and many minor powers possess this land surface. The great powers, territorially considered, may be held to include all owning over a million square miles of land. Since their boundaries are fluctuating and ill defined, especially in South America and Africa, any estimate of their areas must be merely approximate. Hence the following table[5] does not claim

[1] Op. cit., p. 237.
[2] Statesman's Year-Book, 1892, p. xxv.
[3] Petermann's Mittheilungen, Ergänzungsband, xxii, p xi.
[4] Geographisch-statistische Tabellen, 1893, p. 89.
[5] Compiled from the Statesman's Year-Book, 1897.

a high degree of accuracy but still it may serve to make clear the relative position of the United States:

TABLE I.

AREA OF COUNTRIES CONTROLLING OVER ONE MILLION SQUARE MILES.

COUNTRY.	Area in square miles.	Per cent. of earth's surface.
British Empire	11,334,391	21.7
Russian Empire	8,660,282	16.5
Chinese Empire	4,218,401	8.1
United States	3,607,950	6.9
Brazil	3,209,878	6.1
France[1]	2,804,839	5.4
Argentine Republic	1,778,195	3.4
Ottoman Empire[1]	1,609,240	3.1
German Empire[1]	1,228,740	2.3
Total	38,451,916	73 5

Among these nine great powers one is purely Asiatic, three purely American, and five inter-continental; but in their origin seven are European and from present indications the two non-European empires of China and Turkey are tottering. The table thus illustrates both the control of European civilization and governments over the world and the preëminent position territorially of a small number of states. Among these great powers the United States ranks fourth and exercises jurisdiction over between one-fifteenth and one-fourteenth of the earth's land surface.

In the United States exclusive of Alaska, where no such measurements have been completed, there are about 17,200 square miles of coast waters, 14,500 square miles of rivers and 75,250 square miles of lakes.[2] The Great

[1] Including extensive African possessions.
[2] Tenth Census, Bulletin, The Areas of the United States, etc., p. 5.

Lakes include over two-thirds of the lake area of the country. As the land surface is 2,970,000 square miles, about 3½ per cent. of the entire area is water. On the average in each ten thousand square miles of total area there are 56 square miles of coast waters, 47 square miles of rivers, and 245, or excluding the Great Lakes, 79 square miles of lakes.

A division conventional and temporary rather than natural, but important for the census, is that between Indian reservations and the rest of the country. Different agencies were employed to count their inhabitants, including the residents of Indian territory and Alaska. In 1890 there were 180,884 square miles of reservations, or 6 per cent. of the area of the country.[1] Their extent, however, is rapidly decreasing. Between 1890 and 1896 they decreased to 130,320 square miles, or nearly 28 per cent.[2]

The United States, exclusive of purely national territory, namely, the Great Lakes, Delaware, Raritan and lower New York bays, is divided into fifty-one political divisions, of which forty-four at the date of the last census were states.[3] The Yellowstone National Park and No Man's Land are apparently included for purposes of measurement within state bounds. Messrs. Gannett and Carpenter have measured the area of each state ex-

---

[1] Eleventh Census, Indians, p. 91.

[2] Report of the Commissioner of Indian Affairs, 1896. p. 495.

[3] For the sake of brevity the word state or states will be applied henceforth, unless otherwise indicated, to all primary divisions of the country including Alaska, Arizona, Indian, New Mexico, Oklahoma and Utah territories and the District of Columbia.

cept Alaska in the manner already explained[1] and adjusted the results to that obtained for the country. But as their boundaries have been surveyed and mapped less accurately than the national boundary and in certain instances, *e. g.*, between Virginia and West Virginia, are very ill ascertained, the area of a state may be deemed, in nearly every case, less accurate than that of the country. Colorado, Wyoming and Utah, being bounded entirely by parallels or meridians, are exceptions. In the table on page 218, in which the states are arranged in order of size, it will be noticed that the numbers expressing the areas of the states all end in a cipher or a five. Hence they cannot be accurate to a square mile. In a personal letter from which I am permitted to quote, Mr. Gannett says : " The areas cannot be given with such accuracy as to make it worth while

---

[1] *Sources.*—The areas of the United States, of the states and territories, and of the counties and parishes, at the date of the 11th census, are stated in Census Bulletin 23, dated Jan. 21, 1891, and prepared "primarily for the use of the Census Office." The Bulletin gives the gross area, the land surface, and the water surface of the primary divisions of the country, and the land surface of each county and parish, except in the case of Oklahoma. It is apparently the standard authority for the area of the United States, its figures are repeated in standard English and Continental publications, and I am not acquainted with any independent determinations of area for the whole country with which its results may be compared.

The area of each city of over 10,000 inhabitants was asked on the schedule of questions relating to the social statistics of cities, and the areas of fifty of these cities have been published in Census Bulletin 100, Social Statistics of Cities.

The areas of the states of Massachusetts, Rhode Island, Connecticut and New Jersey, and of their counties and towns, townships or boroughs, as they stood about 1890, have been published in recent bulletins of the United States Geological Survey, numbers 115–118.

to give the unit figures exactly excepting in the case of
two or three states, and rather than give an incorrect
impression of accuracy, I judged it best to round them
up to the nearest five or ten square miles."

The water surface of each state except Alaska has
been approximately determined under the categories of
lakes, rivers and coast waters.[1] From these measurements the proportion of each kind of water surface to
the whole area of the state has been computed and is
also included in the table on the following page.

On examining the second column two gaps in the
series may be noticed between Georgia and Washington
and between Maryland and West Virginia. All states
above Missouri are larger than the average for the
country, which is 69,723 square miles, and Missouri and
Washington are larger than the average for the country,
exclusive of Alaska. The states then fall into three
groups of large, medium and small. All states with
more than 60,000 square miles lie west of the Mississippi,
and including Alaska cover over nine-tenths of that
region. All with less than 15,000 square miles except
Vermont touch the Atlantic north of the Potomac. The
medium sized states lie between the small and the large.
The large states include 68 per cent. of the country's area,
the medium states, 30.5 per cent. and the small states
about 1.5 per cent. The third column in Table II shows
where the largest proportion of lake surface is found.
The most extensive lake region is in the vicinity of the
Great Lakes. From Minnesota to the Atlantic every

[1] Tenth Census, Bulletin, The Areas of the United States, etc., p. 4.

TABLE II.

GROSS AREA OF THE STATES AND PROPORTION OF COAST WATER, LAKE AND RIVER SURFACE.

STATES.	Gross area.	Square Miles in 10,000 of area.			
		Lake.	River.	Coast waters.	Total.
Alaska	531,000 ( )	?	?	?	?
Texas	265,780	7	30	95	132
California	158,360	100	15	34	149
Montana	146,080	25	28	. . . .	53
New Mexico	122,580	. . . .	9	. . . .	9
Arizona	113,020	2	7	. . . .	9
Nevada	110,700	84	3	. . . .	87
Colorado	103,925	1	26	. . . .	27
Wyoming	97,890	23	9	. . . .	32
Oregon	96,030	96	52	5	153
Utah	84,970	318	9	. . . .	327
Idaho	84,800	38	24	. . . .	62
Minnesota	83,365	456	43	. . . .	499
Kansas	82,080	. . . .	46	. . . .	46
South Dakota	77,650	?	?	. . . .	103
Nebraska	77,510	5	82	. . . .	87
North Dakota	70,795	?	?	. . . .	85
Missouri	69,415	7	92	. . . .	99
Washington	69,180	52	81	200	333
Georgia	59,475	8	51	25	84
Michigan	58,915	208	44	. . . .	252
Florida	58,680	384	67	307	858
Illinois	56,650	24	91	. . . .	115
Wisconsin	56,040	209	75	. . . .	284
Iowa	56,025	21	73	6	100
Arkansas	53,850	49	100	. . . .	149
Alabama	52,250	2	84	84	170
North Carolina	52,250	33	48	625	706
New York	49,170	183	61	71	315
Louisiana	48,720	350	111	218	679
Mississippi	46,810	21	73	6	100
Pennsylvania	45,215	7	44	. . . .	51
Virginia	42,450	6	123	420	549
Tennessee	42,050	24	48	. . . .	72
Ohio	41,060	39	34	. . . .	73
Kentucky	40,400	6	93	. . . .	99
Oklahoma	39,030	?	?	. . . .	51
Indiana	36,350	30	91	. . . .	121
Maine	33,040	697	91	165	943
Indian territory	31,400	?	?	. . . .	127
South Carolina	30,570	2	59	71	133
West Virginia	24,780	. . . .	55	. . . .	55
Maryland	12,210	. . . .	410	1515	1925
Vermont	9,565	398	52	. . . .	450
New Hampshire	9,305	237	86	86	409
Massachusetts	8,315	108	72	151	331
New Jersey	7,815	45	154	262	461
Connecticut	4,990	80	160	50	290
Delaware	2,050	. . . .	291	146	437
Rhode Island	1,250	160	80	1080	1320
District of Columbia	70	. . . .	1429	. . . .	1429
United States[1]	3,076,950	245	47	56	348

[1] Excluding Alaska and the sea within the three mile limit but including Delaware, Raritan and lower New York bays and this country's portion of the Great Lakes.

state on the northern boundary of the country except
Ohio, and every New England state except Connecticut,
has over one per cent. of its area in lakes. The same is
true of Florida, Louisiana, California and Utah. From the
fourth column it appears that the largest proportion of
river surface is found along the Atlantic coast in Connecticut, New Jersey, Delaware, Maryland and Virginia,
and also in the lower Mississippi valley, in Arkansas
and Louisiana, each of these states having over one per
cent. of river surface.

The states which had over five per cent. of their area
in Indian reservations in 1890 were :

States.	Per cent. of area in Indian reservations.
Indian territory	100
Oklahoma	48
South Dakota	47
New Mexico	13
Montana	11
Washington	9
Minnesota	9
Arizona	9
Utah	8
North Dakota	7
Idaho	5

It will be seen that they lie mainly west of the
Mississippi along the northern and southern boundaries
of the country.

In the census volumes [1] the fifty states of the Union
excluding Alaska are divided into five geographical

[1] See for example the Abstract of the Eleventh Census, second edition, p. 10. The student should have this excellent hand-book at his
side. References will be made to it, rather than to the large volumes,
wherever possible.

groups, the north Atlantic, south Atlantic, north central, south central and western. The primary line of division is perhaps that between the Rocky Mountain and Pacific Coast states and those lying east of the great plateau. It follows the meridian of 104 degrees west, *i. e.*, the western boundary of the Dakotas, or the state boundary nearest thereto. It also coincides roughly with the line of 5,000 feet of altitude. Only a trifling part of the area to the east of it rises above that elevation, while fully half of the land to the west is more than that height above the sea level.

The states east of this line are divided upon geographic, historic and economic grounds into north and south. The division is made by a line coinciding in the main with that separating the former slave states from the free states. It follows Mason and Dixon's line, the Ohio river, and the parallel of 36 degrees 30 minutes, or the state line nearest to that, until it intersects the division line between the central and western states. Missouri is thus classed with the north and Oklahoma with the south. Each of the southern states as thus defined, except West Virginia and Oklahoma, has over ten per cent. of negroes in its population, while this is true of no northern state.

The last division, that between the Atlantic and the central states, follows as nearly as the state lines allow the height of land separating the two drainage areas but is invariably somewhat to the west of this natural division. West Virginia is the only exception. While most of the state sends its rainfall to the Ohio river it is classed for historic reasons among the Atlantic states, and while it has a smaller proportion of negroes than any other southern state, or than Missouri of the northern, it is classed for the same reason among the southern states.

With the exception of the District of Columbia and Alaska, each of the fifty-one primary divisions of the country is subdivided territorially. In 1890 there were about twenty-eight hundred (2790) of these subdivisions, or counties as they are almost uniformly called. This includes the District of Columbia, the parishes of Louisiana, the six reservations of Indian territory, and two parcels of unorganized territory about the size of counties, one in North Dakota and one in Nebraska. For the sake of brevity all these secondary divisions will henceforward be called counties. The average size of a county in the United States is rather more than one thousand (1085) square miles and the range is from Bristol county, Rhode Island, with only twenty-five square miles to Yavapai county, Arizona, over one thousand times as large (29,236 square miles). It is not generally true, however, that the smallest states have the smallest counties. On the contrary the smallest counties occur as a rule in the border states east of the Mississippi river where their average size is less than five hundred square miles, as a little computation will readily convince the reader.

The areas of the country and of the states published in connection with the census of 1880 were not changed for the census of 1890. But the areas of the counties were " thoroughly revised "[1] involving a correction on the average of perhaps five per cent., a part of which may have been due to changes during the decade in the location of county boundaries, but more to increased accuracy of measurement. The method of measurement resembled that employed for the country and the states : that is, the area of each state was the starting point and the county areas, determined primarily by the polar planimeter, were corrected by a reference to the requisite total ; but as the mapping of county lines is generally less accurate than that of state boundaries, the probable error in county areas is greater. Mr. Gannett writes me : " Excepting where we have accurate maps of county boundaries, the areas given can be regarded only as very rough approximations and this is true in all the eastern states and especially so in those of the south where the location of county boundaries is not represented alike upon any two maps."

In Rhode Island, where the Geological Survey also has determined the land surface of the counties, the results of the two are comparable, and show an average variation of six per cent.[2] The results of the Geological Survey in New Jersey were the basis of the census figures, and in Massachusetts and Connecticut the former gives the gross area, not the land surface. If both were accurate in the latter states, the Geological Survey figures would form a maximum limit not exceeded in any

[1] Eleventh Census, Bulletin 23, p. 1. Compare Tenth Census, Bulletin, The Areas of the U. S., etc.

[2] The land surface of the counties of Rhode Island is given as follows in the two authorities :

case by those of the census. In fact the land surface of
eight of the twenty-two counties is stated by the census
bulletin as greater than their gross area indicated by
the Geological Survey, a proof of not a little inaccuracy
in one or the other.[1]

Such discrepancies have made it seem worth while to
attempt a determination of the probable error in the
official census statement of county areas. The simplest
method to follow would be a repetition of planimetric
measurements on our most accurate county maps, the
United States post route maps. This method has already been employed by a German critic and the results
in three cases published,[2] but it is obviously open to the
objection that in those maps the county lines may have
been inaccurately drawn. Far more accurate than those
are the maps of the United States Coast and Geodetic
Survey and of the United States Lake Survey, but these
latter represent only natural not political divisions and

COUNTIES.	Geological Survey Bulletin.	Census Bulletin 23.	Per cent. of variation.
Bristol	25	25	0
Kent	169	180	7
Newport	117	100	15
Providence	411	440	7
Washington	331	340	3
Total	1,053	1,085	

[1] For example the Survey bulletin gives the gross area of Berkshire
county, Mass., as 942 and of Norfolk county, Mass., as 433 square
miles, while the census gives the land surface alone of the same
counties as 959 and 494 square miles.

[2] Cf. Petermann's Geographische Mittheilungen, Ergänzungsbände
17-18, No. 84, p. 4, footnote.

include only our boundary districts. There are, however, six cases in which natural divisions between land and water coincide with county lines ; in other words along the boundary of the United States there are six islands or groups of islands which are also counties. They are Nantucket, Martha's Vineyard, Long island, Staten island, Isle Royale and Beaver, Fox and Manitou islands. Long island is divided into three counties, and is the only island containing more than one. The areas of these counties on the Coast Survey or Lake Survey charts have been twice measured carefully by Mr. J. F. Hayford, C.E., formerly of the United States Coast Survey and now of Cornell university, and from his results I have prepared the following table :

TABLE III.

COMPARISON OF MEASURED LAND SURFACE OF CERTAIN COUNTIES IN SQUARE MILES WITH CENSUS FIGURES.

COUNTY AND STATE.	ISLAND OR GROUP.	Meas-ured area.	Area by Census Bulletin, 1880.	Area by Census Bulletin, 1890.	Area by other authorities.	Per Cent. of variation of census 1890 area from measurement.
Dukes, Mass.	Martha's Vineyard.	103.4	120	124	110*	20
Nantucket, "	Nantucket. .	49.7	60	65	51*	31
Kings, Queens and Suffolk, New York .	Long island .	1353.8	1110	1007	1682†	25
Richmond, New York.	Staten island.	55.7	60	61	59†	10
Manitou, Mich.	Beaver, Fox and Manitou	109.3	200	120	. . . .	10
Isle Royale, Mich.	Isle Royale .	203.7	230	215	. . . .	5

* U. S. Geological Survey, Bulletin 116.

† New York Census of 1875, p. 264.

If these instances were typical, the county areas in Census Bulletin 23 were in error by an average amount of 17 per cent. But the north central and western states are probably better mapped and measured than these results would indicate. It should also be remarked that in four of the six cases the changes made in 1890 resulted in greater inaccuracy than before. It has surprised me to find that the area of Long island, perhaps the largest and certainly the most important island in the country, has not been determined to within twenty-five per cent. The latest Federal authority, as appears from the preceding table, gives it as 1007 square miles, while what is I believe the latest state authority, the state census of 1875, basing itself directly upon Hough's Gazetteer and ultimately upon French's Gazetteer of 1860, gives its area as 1682 square miles. The latter is the authority followed by such good secondary sources as the last editions of the Encyclopædia Britannica and Johnson's Cyclopædia. It will be seen that the state and Federal authorities differ by over six hundred and fifty square miles and that each is over three hundred miles wide of the truth as first established by Mr. Hayford's measurements. [1]

[1] To illustrate the care with which his work has been done I append his report to me on the measurement of the area of Long island. The map from which his measurements were made was the Coast and Geodetic Survey Chart, No. 52, "Montauk Point to New York." It will be seen that his two determinations differ by less than a fourth of one per cent. He is confident that the errors of measurement as distinguished from the errors of the map are well within one per cent.

LINCOLN HALL, April 29, 1896.

Prof. W. F. Willcox :

DEAR SIR—By the use of the polar planimeter on the C. & G. S.

The census makes no general effort to determine the area of divisions smaller than counties, except in the case of large cities. The areas of fifty of these are stated in one of the bulletins and assurance is given that they "have been either determined by actual measurements from latest obtainable maps or from records in offices of the several city engineers."[1] The areas of nearly all the cities and towns of Massachusetts, Rhode Island, Connecticut and New Jersey are given in recent bulletins of the United States Geological Survey. Eleven of the fifty cities included in Census Bulletin 100 are in these four states and six other cities are co-extensive with counties of the same name. Hence for one-third of the fifty cities there are two independent and comparable determinations of area. The general result

map which you furnished, I have obtained the following results. Long island was for convenience divided into seven sections, arbitrarily, and the area of each section measured twice.

No. of Section.	Sq. stat. miles 1st measurement.	Sq. stat. miles 2d measurement.
1	129 6	127.2
2	246.6	246.1
3	334.1	335.2
4	9.0	9.9
5	287.1	286.4
6	253.9	256.2
7	95.1	91.2
Total area	1355.4	1352.2

Mean of two measurments = 1353.8 sq. miles.

The method used eliminates the effect of the shrinkage of the paper on which the map was printed,—each portion of the area being compared with the area of the circumscribing rectangle formed by printed meridians and parallels.   Yours respectfully,

                                              JOHN F. HAYFORD.

[1] Eleventh Census, Bulletin 100, p. 5.

of a comparison is to reveal occasional discrepancies too wide to be due to variations of measurement ; *e. g.*, St. Louis 48 and 61 square miles, San Francisco 50 and 15, New Orleans 187 and 37, Holyoke 4 and 18. An explanation is found in the fact that for the bulletin on the Social Statistics of Cities only the built up area of certain cities was measured. This fact is not stated in the bulletin itself but has been authoritatively admitted to me in correspondence. As there is no way to decide for what cities it is true, it is impossible to accept the careful measurements in that bulletin since we can not tell what area was measured. Still it may be mentioned that among the populous cities of the country there are apparently only two of great area, Chicago and Philadelphia. They are said to include respectively 161 and 129 square miles, while the third in size, St. Louis, contains only 61, and New York only 40 square miles.

The preceding analysis points to the conclusion that owing primarily to the inaccurate or incomplete surveys upon which reliance must often be placed, the determinations of area of the United States, and of its political divisions large and small, are not to be accepted without hesitation. It may serve also as an example of a kind of interpretative criticism which, although perhaps impracticable under past conditions, would be extremely desirable from the compilers and editors of our official statistics. They could prepare it more easily and accurately than a private individual unfamiliar with the processes by which statistical results have been secured. Notwithstanding these reasons for its inclusion, so detailed a criticism of what is merely preliminary to the study of social statistics would hardly be in place, were it not hoped that it would conduce to awaken in the beginner an attitude of independent inquiry and a refusal to accept on authority any fact which may be made for him to rest on a better foundation. Such an attitude is an indispensable prerequisite to the successful study of statistics and one difficult to establish in an untrained mind.

CHAPTER II.

The word population means the number of living human beings. Yet along with this, its usual present meaning, there occurs a secondary one of importance in the history of political economy and statistics, viz., increase in the number of human beings. While the classical writers on political economy use the word in both senses or equivocally, in the title and pages of Malthus's Principle of Population, and in the discussions it has aroused, emphasis is laid upon the idea of increase. Light is thrown upon this double meaning by the history of the word. While Bacon employed it in substantially its present meaning, it seems not to have become current in the European languages until the last century, and then often if not usually with the active sense of increase more or less clearly marked. [1] This meaning of population, like the original meaning of statistics, is now of importance only to the historian or the critic.

[1] Its use in this active sense during the latter half of the last century may be illustrated by the following quotations from German, French, English and American sources :

1761 : Suessmilch, The population (*Bevölkerung*) of a state as a duty of its ruler.

1772 : Raynal, The surest proof of the population (*population*) of the human species is the depopulation of other species.

1776 : Declaration of Independence, He has endeavored to prevent the population of these states.

1798 : Malthus, Rapid population.

As the number of human beings is variable in time, increasing with births and decreasing with deaths, the concept must be limited by a reference to some definite point or period of time. By the last census of the United States the time was fixed as the first day of June, 1890. All inhabitants living on that day and no others were enumerated. Concerning the manner in which the several thousand persons born or dying on that day were to be entered no instructions were given to the enumerators. The foreign practice is to make a census speak as of a certain moment, commonly midnight, of the enumeration day, and the practice is theoretically preferable to our own. The concept must be limited also in space to a certain country or part of a country. In the case of area the whole is known better than its parts, and is the standard by reference to which the parts are corrected; in the present subject the primary datum is the population of the parts from which that of the whole is laboriously and imperfectly constructed. But in defining population with reference to any part of the earth's surface, difficulties at once arise from the mobility of human beings.

The population of a country having a census is merely the sum of the populations of the districts into which it is divided for enumeration and each of these in the United States is supposed ordinarily to contain about four thousand inhabitants. [1] Hence the basal definition is that of the population not of a country,

[1] "The subdivision assigned to any enumerator shall not exceed four thousand inhabitants as near as may be, according to estimates based on the Tenth Census." Census Law of March 1, 1889, § 12.

state, county or city, but of an enumeration district. By what criterion shall an enumerator on his round decide whether any person he meets belongs to the population of his district? The International Statistical Congress at St. Petersburg in 1872, in voting that general censuses of population should include all persons present in the enumerator's district at the moment to which the census relates, offered an answer to the question, which has the advantage of furnishing the enumerator with a simple test question, "Were you in my district, *i. e.*, within certain known boundaries, at a certain recent moment?" This is now the method almost universally followed in Europe. But where it is employed the census must be taken with great speed, the common European practice being to complete the primary enumeration within twenty-four hours, and it is doubtful whether such expedition would be practicable under American conditions. At present the field work in the national census may by law occupy two weeks in a city of over ten thousand people and a month elsewhere,[1] and in practice does not fall much within that.

While under the terms of the constitution of the United States[2] the census is to include "the whole number of persons in each state excluding Indians not taxed," Congress has uniformly interpreted the word "numbers," or the phrase, "persons in each state," to mean the inhabitants rather than the persons physically present in each district, and the states have followed the same prac-

[1] Ibid., § 19.

[2] Amendments, Article xiv, § 2. Compare Constitution, Art. I, § 2.

tice. Each enumerator, accordingly, must take oath that he will count all the inhabitants of his district,[1] and the implied test of inhabitancy is having one's "usual place of abode"[2] in the district. In explanation of this ambiguous phrase the Instructions to Enumerators at the last census says: "It is difficult to afford administrative directions which will wholly obviate the danger that some persons will be reported in two places and others not reported at all. Much must be left to the judgment of the enumerator," (p. 21). As the latter may wish to show that his district or city compares favorably with that of others and as his pay depends upon the number of names secured rather than on the hours worked,[3] he may be expected to include on his schedules most of the doubtful cases which come to his knowledge. This consideration raises the large and difficult problem of the accuracy of the census of 1890.

This Study is based upon the Eleventh Census and yet, as already shown in the previous chapter, the entire trustworthiness of that basis cannot be assumed. Neither can it be proved at the outset. On the contrary it must be accepted as a working hypothesis to be constantly tested and if necessary corrected or rejected as the results of investigation require. The ability to probe a census and to form an independent and reasoned judgment upon its accuracy is perhaps as high evidence as can be given that one has served his apprenticeship to the statistical

[1] Census Law, § 8.

[2] Ibid., § 9.

[3] Ibid., § 11.

method and mastered it. Hence at the start only a few general suggestions are in place.

A census is not a unit or an organic whole, but a collection and interpretation of the answers to a long series of questions set all over a country and to all classes of society. The answers vary in accuracy with the region and social class from which they come, and with the character of the question asked. Answers from Massachusetts or Rhode Island, where regular and careful state censuses contribute to maintain a statistical tradition among the people, are more trustworthy than answers from New Mexico. Answers from whites are probably more correct than answers from negroes. A citizen will give the place of his birth more correctly on the average than the information whether he is a pauper or a sufferer from chronic disease. Hence finding the accuracy of a census is not a single or simple problem, but can result only from finding the accuracy with which each question was answered and balancing the results. Rarely if ever is a census so ill taken that no conclusions are to be derived from a critical use of its figures; rarely if ever is one so well taken that all it contains may be accepted without criticism and at its face value.

But the number of people in a country is the primary fact derived from a census and therefore to dispute a census is commonly and naturally understood to apply to that alone. After the trustworthiness of this result has been investigated, however, that of every other return on which inference or argument is based should be made, if possible, the theme of a separate study, a requisite not infrequently ignored, but one on which unfortunate experience leads me to insist.

Errors may creep into a census through blunders of the public, of the enumerators, or of the central office. Blunders of the public are either ignorant or wilful. Of the persons visited some are unable to answer the questions put to them. Many would not know their "age at nearest birthday". Many who would be offended by doubt of their ability to answer so plain a question would give their age at the last birthday; of such replies about half must be wrong. Unwillingness to answer is a more serious cause of error than inability. Many persons born abroad, would return themselves as native. Some would be unwilling to admit service in the Confederate army, others the mixture of negro blood, others that they were divorced, others inability to read or write. But perhaps the questions which at the Eleventh Census aroused most widespread dissatisfaction, and were probably answered with least correctness, were those in reference to acute or chronic diseases, bodily or mental defects, delinquency or dependency. The accuracy of answers to these questions must be established or the results treated as giving merely a minimum. To demand such information tends to arouse in the public mind an antagonism to the entire work which may seriously impair the accuracy of other answers, for its success depends largely upon a public coöperation that is easily forfeited. An active desire to mislead occasionally appears on a large scale, especially in the case of rival cities, in deliberate exaggeration of the number of people. Conspicuous instances at the last census were those of Minneapolis and to a less degree St. Paul; in each a recount was ordered. In these instances the enumerators divided the responsibility with the public.

The errors of enumerators are likely to vary, first, with the character of the men and this probably with the method of their appointment, secondly, with the lucidity and detail of their instructions and the means taken to secure a mastery of those instructions before the field work begins, thirdly, with the care and success with which the field work is superintended, and fourthly, with the method of their payment.

The errors of the central office are either clerical mistakes in copying or tabulating results, a large proportion of which are discovered and corrected in the progress of the work, or errors of analysis and interpretation of results. The former class are usually beyond detection by the private student, but fortunately are seldom of material importance; the latter are sometimes serious and misleading.

Prior to the commencement of work on the Eleventh Census the attitude of the public towards such statistical work was probably more favorable than ever before. The rapid dissemination of elementary education had been helpful. Statistical arguments and with them a realization of the importance of statistics had become more common. More states than previously had taken censuses of their own and so educated the public to expect such questions. The appointment of the superin-

tendent of the Eleventh Census, however, was not received with as general and deep popular satisfaction as
that of his predecessor, General Francis A. Walker.
Upon the results of a census depend the distribution of
seats and possibly the balance of power in the House of
Representatives. A department which has to furnish
the facts upon which the decision of these questions is
based should be as free from suspicion of partizan bias
as the Supreme Court, and the work of a census officer is
probably more completely separable from politics than
is that of a judge. However high the qualifications of
the superintendent of the Eleventh Census for his position may have been, he had not at the time of his appointment earned a national reputation as an impartial statistician at all comparable with that of his
predecessor. He was known to have done much work
for leading newspapers of his political party. I cannot
but think, therefore, that the appointment did not
deepen the popular faith that the approaching census
would be accurate and impartial, and such faith is almost
an indispensable prerequisite of thoroughly satisfactory
work. Further doubt and opposition were aroused in
certain quarters by the failure to employ competitive
examinations in selecting subordinate employees.
Whether the responsibility rested upon Congress which
passed the law or upon some one or more of the executive officers who carried it into effect is immaterial to
my contention. The claim that the methods employed
in the Tenth Census were being followed did not dis-
arm the criticism ; the civil service law had been passed

in the interim and public opinion had altered. Evidence was offered in the press that enumerators were appointed at the suggestion of party leaders.[1] The supervisor of the New York city district was charged with the appointment of about eight hundred enumerators. A prominent metropolitan paper printed a circular letter alleged to have been sent by him to local Republican politicians and reading as follows : " Dear Sir : Will you please forward to this office the list of applicants that the Republican organization of your district desires to have named as census enumerators ? "[2] Statements were published that some enumerators were unable to read or write,[3] that others had their photographs in the Rogues' Gallery.[4] The circulation of such assertions whether true or false could not but impair the popular confidence in the census.

Evidence of careful supervision of the work, however, is offered by the instructions sent out to the forty thousand enumerators connected with the census. They fill a pamphlet of 46 pages, are more than twice the length of the instructions issued for the preceding census and show in many ways an advance in lucidity and detail. No light has been found upon the question whether the enumerators were compelled to master these instructions before entering upon their duties or whether their reports day by day were carefully scrutinized to insure conform-

[1] Civil Service Record, April, 1891, p. 102.

[2] Nation, 51 : 224.

[3] Civil Service Record, August, 1890, p. 12.

[4] Letter of W. D. Foulke, N. Y. Daily Times, Nov. 15, 1890, p. 5.

ity. They were paid usually at the rate of two cents
for each name returned, but in sparsely settled districts
somewhat more. [1] This method of payment, while
tempting the enumerator to include all doubtful names
even at the risk of double enumeration, also invites him
to pass by those whom it is more than two cents' worth
of trouble to reach.

The methods of impeaching a census may be grouped
into four classes :

1. It may be proved that faults existed either in the
census law or in the organization or administration of
the working force and that their inevitable or natural
result would be serious inaccuracies of enumeration. 2.
Inferences logically drawn from different parts of a census
may prove to be irreconcilable. 3. The results may be
compared with those obtained by another count, which
was taken at about the same time and proved to be
more accurate. 4. The results may be compared with
those of a series of enumerations before and after the one
in question, on the assumption that a general uniformity
in the rate of change should appear and that any wide
and unexplained variation from it is evidence of error.
These lines of attack find partial illustration in the arguments by which all critics have been convinced that
serious errors crept into the Ninth Census and that the
Tenth was more correct than any previous one. After
years of attempted administration of the law of 1850, under which the Ninth Census was taken, General Walker
pointed out its faults. It laid the supervision of the

[1] Census Law, § 11.

enumeration in each district upon an officer already bur-
dened with other duties and gave the census office no
control over him. Under such circumstances, the office
disclaimed responsibility for the results reported. [1] And
again, when the results of the census of 1880 in parts of
the south indicated an incredible increase of population
in the preceding decade, a recount was ordered in some
localities with results uniformly confirming the later and
discrediting the earlier enumeration.

In all these four ways critics have sought to impeach
the Eleventh Census. A brief summary of the conclusions to which I have been brought with my reasons for
holding them is here presented.

The law under which the last census was taken is substantially a re-enactment or the law of 1879. Of the
earlier law General Walker said in his official report,
written after he had been administering its provisions
for six months : " The legislation of the last Congress
on the subject of the census was wise and salutary. Not
a single fundamental defect in the scheme of enumeration has appeared. " [2] The superintendent of the Eleventh
Census called to his aid many of the most valued assistants
at the previous count. He says : " Five-sixths of all the
experts and chiefs had experience in the Tenth Census," [3]
and that sixteen of the twenty-five divisions were in
charge of the same men who were over them in 1880. [4]

[1] Report of Superintendent of Census. Tenth Census, Compendium,
Part I, p. ix.

[2] Ibid., p. xxxiv.

[3] Eleventh Census, Compendium, Part I, p. xxxii.

[4] R. P. Porter, Partisanship and the Census. North American Rev.,
151 : 662.

Over against these facts should be set two charges which, in my opinion, have not been adequately met, first, that the career and published work of Mr. Porter were not those of an independent and judicial statistician and, secondly, that in the appointment of enumerators and other subordinates, there is reason to believe that the letter and spirit of the census law requiring enumerators to be " selected solely with reference to fitness and without reference to their political party affiliations, " [1] were less strictly interpreted and enforced in 1890 than in 1880. In addition to the evidence already cited upon this point, I am allowed to quote the following from a personal letter written to me in 1896 by Dr. John Shaw Billings, who was in charge of the division of Vital Statistics at the Eleventh Census :

" The whole of my work in the census has been done in the face of great obstacles, owing to repeated changes of clerks for political reasons, etc., and I am tired of struggling with the most unpropitious circumstances which have surrounded the work." It seems probable that the law under which the Eleventh Census was taken was better than any prior to 1879, but that its administration was somewhat inferior to that of the Tenth Census.

Arguments based upon the apparent inconsistency of different parts of the census are best presented in connection with the topics to which they relate and their consideration is, therefore, postponed.

Recounts of the entire population occurred, so far as

[1] Laws of 1879 and 1889, § 5.

I have ascertained, in the case of four cities, St. Paul and Minneapolis, Minn., Helena, Mont., and Portland, Ore. In each case important errors were discovered either before or during the recount. Partial recounts were ordered in other places with results confirming the figures originally given to the public.

The fourth and most important method of attack is not yet fully possible. It was not until the results of the census of 1880 were published and confirmed that those of the Ninth Census were generally discredited, and the best test of the correctness of the Eleventh Census will be the degree to which it conforms to the Twelfth and subsequent counts.

The recent appearance of the results of many state censuses, however, permits a partial application of this line of criticism. The method employed in such a test is to assume that the population of a state was correctly enumerated at the censuses next before and after that of 1890, and from these two fixed points to compute what it was at that date. Wide and frequent variations between such estimates and the results of the Eleventh Census would be suspicious. General agreement between them would be strong proof of the accuracy of the disputed facts. Close and constant correspondence is not to be anticipated.

In order to apply this test, I have sent a circular letter to the secretary of state of each state in which, either from the recent report of the Commissioner of Labor upon a plan for a permanent census bureau[1], or from the World

[1] Fifty-fourth Congress, Second Session, Senate Document, No. 5, p. 11, (December, 1896).

Almanac for 1897,[1] I had reason to believe that an enumeration had been made since 1890. The letter asked for the year and month of the state census and for the total population enumerated, but in many replies only the year was stated. In those cases I have assumed that the census was taken in June. From the answers the table on the following page has been compiled :[2]

From the figures thus brought together it is possible to compute the population of each state at the date of the Eleventh Census, June, 1890, and to compare the result with the figures in dispute. For this purpose two methods are in use, the arithmetical and the geometrical, the former assuming that a given population increases by a constant number in a unit of time like a year, and the latter assuming that the population increases by a

[1] Page 378.

[2] The Indiana secretary of state wrote : " No census of the state of Indiana has been made since that of 1890, except that made in April of 1895, giving the voting population of the state." For this reason Indiana, although included in the Commissioner of Labor's list, has been omitted. Oklahoma and South Dakota had no census prior to 1890. No reply was received from the secretary of state of Tennessee. Kansas is omitted because of the confessed incompleteness of the enumeration in 1895. The Oregon census of 1885 has been disregarded because the slight increase it showed over the census of 1880 arouses suspicion that like the last census of Kansas, it was incomplete. The bitter controversy over the accuracy of the Federal enumeration of New York city and Brooklyn in 1890 and the fact that the state enumeration of 1892 was superintended in those cities by persons presumably interested in proving that the national count was seriously deficient have induced me to make a comparison merely for the rest of the state, with reference to which no charges of serious error have been made. The police census of New York city in 1895, however, makes possible an estimate of its population in 1890 by comparing this census with that of 1880, and hence it has been included.

TABLE IV.

POPULATION OF STATES BY CENSUSES TAKEN SINCE 1890.

STATES.	Date of Census.	Population.	Date of Census.	Population.
Florida.	1885	342.617[1]	1895	464,639[2]
Iowa.	1885	1,753,98.[3]	1895	2,058,069[3]
Massachusetts . .	May, 1885	1,942,141[4]	May, 1895	2,500,183[4]
Michigan.	June, 1884	1,853 658[5]	June, 1894	2,241,641[5]
Minnesota	June, 1885	1,117.798[6]	June, 1895	1,574,619[6]
New Jersey. . . .	1885	1,278,033[7]	1895	1,673,106[7]
New York[8] . . .	June, 1880	3,277,077[9]	Feb., 1892	3,716,329[10]
Oregon.	June, 1880	174,768[9]	1895	362,513[11]
Rhode Island. . .	June, 1885	304,284[12]	June, 1895	384.758[2]
Utah	June, 1880	143.963[9]	Feb., 1895	247,324[13]
Wisconsin	1885	1,563.423[14]	1895	1,937,915[2]
New York City . .	June, 1880	1,206,299[9]	Apr., 1895	1,851,060[15]

constant per cent. The difference is like that between simple and compound interest. Each involves an artificial simplification of a complex problem and each applied generally and to long periods of time results in absurdities. No population increases in either way. Non-progressive communities usually do not increase at all and among the most developed communities or

[1] American Almanac, 1889, p. 168.
[2] Personal letter from the secretary of state.
[3] Census of Iowa, 1895, p. 259.
[4] Census of Massachusetts, 1895, Volume I, Part I, p. 23.
[5] Census of Michigan, 1894, Volume I, p. xli.
[6] Census of Minnesota, 1895, p. 65.
[7] Census of New Jersey, 1895, pp. 34, f.
[8] The State excluding New York city and Brooklyn.
[9] Eleventh Census, Compendium, Part I, pp. 32, f.
[10] Census of New York, 1892, pp. 4, f.
[11] Census of Oregon, 1895, p. 11.
[12] Census of Rhode Island, 1885, p. 89.
[13] Census of Utah, 1895, p. 17.
[14] Census of Wisconsin, 1885, p. 38.
[15] Census of New York City, 1895, p. 7.

classes the desire for other elements of wellbeing than
children may bring mankind again to a stationary condition. Between these limits population ordinarily increases with the increase of food, but less rapidly. Mr.
Farr seems to have assumed that because Malthus as-
serted that population tended to increase at a geometrical rate, therefore the formula by which population
should be estimated was that of compound interest.[1] The
assumption was better than the reason on which it was
based. The true justification for the Registrar-General's
method of estimating population is not Malthus's theory of
a tendency, translated as he never translated it into a law
of population, but the fact that the population of England
computed by this method has been nearer to the results
of a careful census than that resulting from a use of the
arithmetical method or any other available. The same
method is to be extended to other countries only after
testing the results of the two and showing its greater
accuracy. There are many considerations pointing to
the conclusion that the rate of increase of population in
the United States now is less than it has been in the
past, and that it will be less in the future than it is now.
For countries with a slowly decreasing rate of increase,
the application of the geometrical method to the determination of the population between two censuses will
give erroneously small results, and under such circumstances the arithmetical method may be the better way
to approximate the facts. It has been shown that this
method would have been somewhat more accurate for

[1] Farr, Vital Statistics, p. 19.

Massachusetts since 1850[1] and for Michigan in recent years,[2] and I am inclined to believe that it corresponds more closely than the other to the present conditions in most of our states. On the other hand the annual number of immigrants between 1890 and 1895 was slightly greater than the number between 1885 and 1890[3] and the excess of births over deaths in Massachusetts and Rhode Island between 1890 and 1894 was larger both absolutely and relatively to the population than between 1885 and 1890.[4] On the whole I slightly prefer the arithmetical method for the United States at present, but in the table on the following page both have been applied.

The censuses and estimates in these tables apply to over twenty-seven per cent. of the total population of the country and the total estimated by one method is within one-half of one per cent. and by the other within one and a half per cent. of the result of the census. But it might be fairer to exclude New York city, where the census of 1890 may have been exceptionally defective and where the difficulties of an accurate count are unparalleled. If this be done the deviation from the esti-

[1] F. S. Crum, The Marriage Rate in Massachusetts, Pub. Am. Stat. Ass'n., 4 : 325, (Dec., 1895).

[2] Michigan Registration Report, 1893, pp. 6-10, and C. L. Wilbur, Note on Methods of Estimating Population, Pub. Am. Stat. Ass'n, 5 : 83-86, June, 1896.

[3] World Almanac, 1897, p. 149.

[4] 27 Report of Mass. State Board of Health, 1895, p. 1 ; 17 Report of R.I. Board of Health, 1894, p. 111. I believe these are the two states whose birth and death rates are most correct.

TABLE V.

COMPARISON BETWEEN RESULTS OF ELEVENTH CENSUS AND
ESTIMATES.

STATES.	Population, June, 1890.			Per cent. of variation from enumerated population of that estimated by	
	Estimated by arithmetical method.	Enumerated.	Estimated by geometrical method.	Arithmetical method	Geometrical method
Florida	403,628	391,422	398,440[1]	+ 3.12	+ 1.92
Iowa	1,906,024	1,911,896	1,882,200	— .31	— 1.55
Massachusetts	2,225,812	2,238,943	2,209,700	— .59	— 1.31
Michigan	2,086,448	2,093,889	2,076,700	— .36	— .82
Minnesota	1,346,208	1,301,826	1,326,600	+3.41	+ 1.90
New Jersey	1,475,569	1,444,933	1,447,200	+2.12	+ .16
New York[2]	3,653,577	3,644,005	3,649,900	+ .26	+ .16
New York city	1,640,969	1,515,301	1,610,000	+8.29	+6.25
Oregon	299,931	313,767	284,320	—4.41	—9.83
Rhode Island . . .	345,521	345,506	342,120	+ .00	— .98
Utah	214,436	207,905	207,990	+3.14	+ .05
Wisconsin	1,750,669	1,686,880	1,740,600	+3.78	+3.18
Total	17,348,792	17,096,273	17,176,270	+ 1.48	+ .47

mates by either method would be well within one per
cent. In other words, assuming (1) that the eleven state
censuses were all accurate ; (2) that the average of these
results may be extended to the remaining three-fourths
of the population of the United States, and (3) that the
population of the whole country has been growing by a
constant amount annually, its true population in June,
1890, was about 63,135,000, and the omissions in the

[1] It will be noticed that the numbers in this column are only approximations. They have been computed with the aid of Fuller's
spiral slide rule. As the error involved will not affect the per cents
in the last column it seemed unnecessary to spend the additional time
necessary for greater accuracy.

[2] Excluding New York city and Brooklyn.

Eleventh Census were rather over half a million, or slightly more than four-fifths of one per cent. On the other hand, if, in accordance with the weight of authority, the assumption that the population has been growing at a constant rate be preferred, then the true population of the United States in June, 1890, was about 62,560,000, and the Eleventh Census reported about 60,000 more people than there were in the country, an error of about one-tenth of one per cent. The only obvious escape from the conclusion is to deny the general accuracy or the typical character of the state censuses, and I see no reason for either. This constitutes a strong argument in favor of the substantial accuracy of the Eleventh Census. Until it is answered or more evidence is presented, the results of that count, it seems to me, must be accepted as more accurate than any estimate which can now be substituted for them. A reader loath to admit a conclusion which has been so often disputed or denied, may attach weight to the opinion of a disinterested expert thoroughly competent to judge. I quote by permission from a letter written to me in July, 1897, by the present head of the Eleventh Census, Carroll D. Wright, Commissioner of Labor. He says : " I think that the Eleventh Census came within less than one per cent. of the true enumeration of the inhabitants. While there was a slight shortage in some cases, this was doubtless in part offset by an unavoidable duplication of names in other parts."

My own opinion has been considerably modified by the study, the conclusions of which have been presented, and I am now convinced that the count is to be accepted. Whatever decision may be reached on the complicated question, critics will probably agree that if the accuracy of the census is to be upheld, it must be on different grounds from the curiously improbable ones stated in the census volumes themselves.[1] They argue that the usual estimate of half to three-fourths of a million for the omissions of the census of 1870 is altogether too small, and that the true population at that time may be better approximated by assuming that " the rate of increase in the southern states between 1860 and 1870 and between 1870 and 1880 was the same." The tacit assumption that the civil war had no perceptible effect upon the decennial increase of population as compared with that of the following decade, is so violent as to arouse the suspicion that the writer was hard pressed for arguments, and the suspicion is confirmed on noticing that the hypothesis is twice denied within the following five pages, but after the necessities of the argument are removed. This may have contributed more than it should to undermine my confidence in a work which appealed to such support. For the foregoing reasons, it is my belief that the Eleventh Census is well within one per cent. of the truth in its statement of the total population of the United States, and that there is little likelihood that now or in the future estimates of greater accuracy can be made.

[1] Eleventh Census. Population, Part I, pp. xi, xii. Compendium, Part I, pp. xxxv–xxxvii.

Statistics has not yet obtained a definite answer to the question, How many people are there on the earth's surface? But much progress has been made in the present century towards its solution. At its beginning the highest careful estimate was probably that of Suessmilch, who had computed it in 1761, as rather more than a billion.[1] In the dearth of better information, he was compelled to guess at the population of Asia by assuming that on the average it was as thickly settled as Europe, and being five times as large, had accordingly five times as many inhabitants.[2] At the present time, the best authorities concur in putting the population of the earth nearly fifty per cent. higher than Suessmilch did.

ESTIMATED POPULATION OF THE EARTH.

AUTHORITY.	Date.	Estimate.
Levasseur [3]	1886	1,483,000,000
Ravenstein [3]	1890	1,467,920,000
Wagner and Supan [3]	1891	1,480,000,000
Juraschek [3]	1893	1,485,763,000

The results of careful and long continued efforts to determine the population of the earth are found in Die Bevölkerung der Erde, and at almost every issue of this work the figure stated as the conclusion of the authors' studies has been an increase on their preceding

[1] His table gives 1,080 million and is followed by the statement, "The entire sum of all persons on the earth's surface accordingly is between 1000 and 1100 million." Die Göttliche Ordnung, ed. 1761, vol. 2, p. 234.

[2] Ibid., p. 215.

[3] Op. cit.

estimates. This will appear from the following summary of their figures in chronological order.

Date.	Estimate.
1866	1350
1872	1377
1874	1391
1875	1397
1876	1424
1878	1439
1880	1456
1882	1434
1891	1480

The causes of the almost uninterrupted increase in the
size of the estimates are an actual increase in the population and the extension of the statistical method. Thus
the number of persons in 1880 who had been either
counted, or, as in Russia, ascertained by many years of
registration, was 626 million.[1] The population of the
same countries in 1891 was 737 million, an increase of
nearly eighteen per cent. Forty-one million of this was
found in Europe and over twelve in the United States,
where it was due to actual increase. Forty-one million
was found in British India, where a considerable part may
have been due to the improved accuracy of the censuses
of 1881 and 1891 over the first Indian census, that of
1871. Since 1880 censuses or careful registrations have
been had for the first time in some of the smaller states
of southeastern Europe, in most of the native states of
India, in Japan and other localities. The combined population of these regions was estimated in 1880 as 85
million; the application of the statistical method showed
it to be 99 million. This method has now been applied

[1] Die Bevölkerung der Erde, 1891, p. vi.

to 836 million people, one-third more than in 1880, and about five-ninths of the estimated population of the earth, but included in this total are the 113 million inhabitants of the Russian Empire, where the first census is now (1897) in progress. A partial offset to this increase in the population of well-governed communities is found in reductions of the estimates for Africa by 38 million and for Asia by 8 million. The greatest open problem is that of the population of China, where two imperfect enumerations have been made during the century, that of 1812 showing 362 million and that of 1842 showing 413 million. The present tendency of critics seems to be in the direction of discarding entirely the results of the later enumeration and assuming that the population has remained stationary or decreased since 1812, but current estimates still differ by nearly 200 million.[1]

It is well-nigh impossible carefully to compare either the area or the population of the continents because there is no concensus regarding their boundaries or the treatment of adjoining islands or polar lands. Hence in both cases the appropriate large unit is the great power, since every nation defines and if possible compels the acceptance of its boundaries. From the standpoint of population the great power may perhaps be defined as one having a population of 35 million or more. In this sense there are probably ten great powers and the number of their inhabitants including those in all dependencies is indicated in the following table:

[1] Op. cit., p. 100.

TABLE VI.

POPULATION OF THE MOST POPULOUS COUNTRIES ACCORDING
TO VARIOUS AUTHORITIES.

COUNTRIES.	Geographisch-statistische Tabellen, 1893.	Almanach de Gotha, 1897.	Statesman's Year-Book, 1897.
China	359,750,000	357,250,000	402,680,000
British Empire . . .	352,374,409	360,800,000	383,488,469
Russian Empire. . . .	116,812,731	121,405,828	129 545,000
France	76,594,435	79,153,192	70,467,775
United States	62,979,766	62,982,244	62,979,766
German Empire . . .	55,658,794	59,353,894	62,879,901
Austria-Hungary . . .	43,233,073	41,384,956	41,358,886
Japan.	40,453,461	41,810,202	41 813,215
Netherlands	36,910,345	39,252,151	38,859,451
Ottoman Empire . . .	21,183,299	36,900,000	39,212,000
Total.	1,165,950,313	1,161,040,317	1,273,284,463

About four-fifths of the inhabitants of the earth are under the sway of some one of these ten great powers. Seven are European in origin and dominant civilization and Christian in religion, Japan is seeking to assimilate or adapt the culture of Europe, while the two other great powers, China and Turkey, are probably stationary or decreasing in population and growing relatively if not absolutely weaker. Among these powers the United States occupies the fifth place and includes about one twenty-fifth of the population of the earth.

It would lead one too far afield to examine the reasons for the differences in the preceding table, but as we are especially concerned with the United States, the figures for their population may be scrutinized in detail. Two of the authorities agree but the third differs by nearly 2,500. The World Almanac for 1897 gives the total population of the United States in 1890 as 62,831,900 [p. 373]. These differences in secondary authorities slight as they are must have some cause. All agree in the basis of the figures, 62,622,250 as the number of residents of the forty-nine states of the Union enumerated in the general count. To this number must be added the population of Alaska, of Indian territory, and of the Indian reservations in other parts of the country. The World Almanac falls into error by ignoring the last of these three additions. But the population of Alaska is given in the World Almanac and at one place in the Tribune Almanac for the current year as 30,329, in the Almanach de Gotha as 31,795 and in the Statesman's Year-Book as 32,052. The first of these numbers is derived from Census Bulletin 30, February 11, 1891, (Alaska, Statistics of Population), which contains a summary of the population as far as then received, 21,929, and adds that 8,400 more will probably come in from remote districts. The second number is taken from Census Bulletin 150, November 28, 1891, (Population of Alaska, Official Count.) The third is derived from the census volume on Alaska published at Washington in 1893. Thus one provisional and two final official statements of the population of Alaska were issued by the Census Office, all different, and apparently no attempt was made to explain their conflict. It is unfortunate to issue provisional and incorrect statements which thus give rise to perpetuated blunders difficult to trace and correct, and in the present case it can scarcely be argued in defense that the people at large or important special interests were waiting impatiently to learn the population of Alaska. The three secondary authorities differ also in their statements of the population of Indian territory, but the source used by the American and German compilations remains undetected. In this case as in the preceding the English manual is correct.

The word population is used in the census volumes in three senses : 1. The constitutional population, which is the basis for the apportionment of members of the House of Representatives. It excludes all residents of territories, the District of Columbia or Indian reservations.[1] 2. The general population, which includes, in addition to the constitutional population, the residents of the District of Columbia and those living off the Indian reservations in all territories except Indian territory and Alaska. 3. The total population, which includes, in addition to the general population, all residents of Indian reservations, Indian territory and Alaska. Of these three meanings, the most commonly employed in the census volumes is the second. For scientific purposes the third is the important one, and hence it is satisfactory to note the suggestion that "it may be advisable hereafter to include in the general population all human beings within the limits of the country whether Indians in tribal relations or otherwise."[2] The constitutional population of the United States June 1, 1890, was 61,908,906 ; the general population was 62,622,250 ; the total population was 62,979,766.

[1] This meaning is very uncommon, but occurs in Compendium, Part I, p. v.

[2] Eleventh Census, Population, Part I, p. c.

While for the country as a whole, the census gives
the total population, for the several states it gives only
the general population. To find their total population
the results of the special Indian census must be added.[1]
In this way the following table has been prepared. The
states are arranged in the order of rank and the proportion that the population of each state makes of the entire population of the country has also been computed
and included.

TABLE VII.

TOTAL POPULATION OF EACH STATE AND PERCENTAGE OF COUNTRY.

STATES.	Population.	Per-centage.	STATES.	Population.	Per-centage.
New York . . .	6,003,174	9.532	West Virginia .	762,794	1.212
Pennsylvania .	5,258,113	8.349	Connecticut . .	746,258	1.185
Illinois	3,826,352	6.076	Maine.	661,086	1.050
Ohio	3,672,329	5.831	Colorado. . . .	413,249	.656
Missouri	2,679,185	4.254	Florida	391,422	.621
Massachusetts .	2,238,947	3.555	New Hampshire	376,530	.598
Texas	2,235,527	3.550	Washington . .	357,232	.567
Indiana	2,192,404	3.481	South Dakota .	348,600	.554
Michigan . . .	2,093,890	3.325	Rhode Island .	345,506	.549
Iowa	1,912,297	3.037	Vermont . . .	332,422	.528
Kentucky . . .	1,858,635	2.952	Oregon . . .	317,704	.505
Georgia	1,837,353	2.917	Dist.of Columbia	230,392	.366
Tennessee . . .	1,767,518	2.807	Utah	210,779	.335
Wisconsin . . .	1,693,330	2.689	North Dakota .	190,983	.303
Virginia	1,655,980	2.630	Indian Territory	180,182	.286
North Carolina	1,617,949	2.569	Delaware . . .	168,493	.268
Alabama . . .	1,513,401	2.403	New Mexico . .	160,282	.255
New Jersey . .	1,444,933	2.294	Montana . .	142,924	.227
Kansas	1,428,108	2.267	Idaho	88,548	.141
Minnesota. .	1,310,283	2.080	Arizona	88,243	.140
Mississippi . .	1,289,600	2.048	Oklahoma . . .	78,475	.125
California . . .	1,213,398	1.927	Wyoming . . .	62,555	.099
South Carolina	1,151,149	1.828	Nevada	47,355	.075
Arkansas . . .	1,128,211	1.791	Alaska	32,052	.051
Louisiana . . .	1,118,588	1.776			
Nebraska . . .	1,062,656	1.687	Total . . .	62,979,766	100.006
Maryland . , .	1,042,390	1.655			

[1] To be found in Eleventh Census, Indians, p. 81.

The table shows that the eight most populous divisions of the country form a belt stretching with but one break, across the country from Massachusetts bay to the Rio Grande. This belt, with Michigan, includes every state with over two million inhabitants, and if Iowa also be added to the list, these ten populous states have over one half of the population of the country. The eight states with least population include, besides Alaska, seven lying in the form of a letter C almost enclosing Colorado and Utah and nowhere touching the coast. They have altogether 700,434 inhabitants, about the same as Maine or Connecticut, and rather more than one per cent. of the population of the entire country. The area they occupy is one and a quarter million (1,245,100) square miles, over two-fifths of the country, or far more than the total area east of the Mississippi. It may also be noticed that only two of the fifty-one states decreased in population in the last decade, and that these were the least populous ones, Nevada and Alaska.

The total population of the counties cannot be known. The results of the special Indian census are given only by states. Hence only the general population of the counties is ascertainable, but as in most of them there are no Indian reservations this fact especially in the eastern states is of little moment. The enumerated population of a county ranges from 3 (in Mackenzie county, North Dakota and Loving county, Texas) to over one and a half million (New York county) and the average population of the 2784 counties outside Indian territory is about 22,500 (22,494).

There are 24 counties, including under that name the District of Columbia, each of which has a population of over two hundred thousand, and 34 each of which has a population of between one and two hundred thousand. Of the former group only one, San Francisco, lies west of the west bank of the Mississippi and only one other, Orleans, lies south of the line of the Potomac and the Ohio. Three-fourths of them touch either the Atlantic or one of the Great Lakes. The populous counties of the country are massed between the Atlantic ocean and the Great Lakes, and the Mississippi, Ohio and Potomac rivers. Of the 58 counties with more than 100,000 inhabitants 49 lie in this region.

But such comparisons as have been implied between the population of different countries, states, or counties may suggest the danger of disregarding the wide differences of area involved. The Netherlands including its East Indian possessions may have about the same population as the Ottoman Empire, or Massachusetts as Texas, or New York as Chicago, but in proportion to the area occupied the two members of each pair differ widely. To avoid the errors likely to arise from overlooking the differences of area, the ratio of population to area or the density of population must be ascertained. Discussion of this subject is reserved for a subsequent study.

Just Ready.

MUNICIPAL PROBLEMS.

BY FRANK J. GOODNOW, LL.D.,

Professor of Administrative Law, Columbia University in the City of New York.

AUTHOR OF "MUNICIPAL HOME RULE," ETC.

Cloth. 16mo. $1.50 net.

Contents :—History of Municipal Organization in the United States.—The Position of the City, as it is, and as it should be. —The Sphere of Municipal Activity.—The Relation of the City to the State.—The Central Administrative Control over Cities in Europe.—The Effects of the Central Administrative Control in England.—Universal Suffrage.—Municipal Government and the National Political Parties.—The City Council.—The City Executive.—The Metropolitan City.

COMMENTS.

" *Municipal Problems* is a scholarly, thoughtful and independent criticism of municipal experiences and the plans now urged to better municipal conditions. . . . The volume is an exceptionally valuable one to close students of municipal affairs."—*The Outlook*, New York.

" This is one of the finest studies in administration that has ever been offered to political students."—*Inter-Ocean*, Chicago.

" We doubt if any author has achieved such eminent success in the solution of the different problems of city government as the author of the present work."—*Times Union*, Albany.

" We know of no single volume so helpful to the student of city governments in the United States at the present time."—*Times-Herald*, Chicago.

" A most useful and timely contribution to the science of municipal government."—*Review of Reviews.*

" This is one of the most important contributions to the literature of this subject here-tofore issued."—*Evening Telegraph*, Philadelphia.

MUNICIPAL HOME RULE,

A Study in Administration.

BY FRANK J. GOODNOW, LL.D.,

Professor of Administrative Law, Columbia University in the City of New York.

Cloth. 16mo. $1.50 net:

COMMENTS.

" We question if any other book before has achieved quite the important service to what may be termed theoretic municipalism. . . . One that all those interested in municipal matters should read. . . . Moderate in tone, sound in argument, and impartial in its conclusions, it is a work that deserves to carry weight."—*London Liberal.*

" Here is without doubt one of the most trenchant and scholarly contributions to political science of recent writing, remarkable for analytical power and lucidity of statement."—*Chicago Evening Post.*

Published for the Columbia University Press by

THE MACMILLAN COMPANY,

66 Fifth Avenue,   **NEW YORK**

Standard Books on Economics.

PUBLISHED BY

THE MACMILLAN COMPANY.

Author's Edition, in Popular Form, with Latest Revisions.

Social Evolution.

By BENJAMIN KIDD. Popular Edition, with the Author's Latest Revisions and New Copyright Preface. Price in paper 25 cents, cloth $1.50.

"The volume . . . owes much of its success to its noble tone, its clear and delightful style, and to the very great pleasure the reader experiences as he is conducted through the strong, dignified and courteous discussion. From a scientific point of view it is the most important contribution recently made to biological sociology.—*Independent.*

An Introduction to Social Philosophy.

By JOHN S. MACKENZIE, M.A., B.A., Assistant Lecturer on Philosophy in Owens College, Manchester, formerly Examiner in Philosophy in the University of Glasgow. 8vo. $2.60.

". . . The ideal depends upon three elements—individual culture, the subjugation of nature, and social organization ; and true progress must include progress in all three. The details of this progress are worked out in a suggestive and interesting manner, and the whole discussion is marked with scholarship as well as good sense.—*Independent.*

The Principles of Sociology. (*Third edition.*)

An Analysis of the Phenomena of Association and of Social Organization. By FRANKLIN HENRY GIDDINGS, M.A., Professor of Sociology in Columbia University. Cloth. 8vo. Price $3.00, *net.*

"A valuable treatise which will, we believe, for many years to come, be *the* text-book on this subject.—*The New Unity.*

"The book is especially valuable because of the clearness and fulness with which it discusses the psychical elements in social evolution.—EDWARD M. COLIE in *The Bookman.*

The Theory of Socialization.

A Syllabus of the Principles of Sociology. By F. H. GIDDINGS, M.A. With references to "The Principles of Sociology," by the same author. 8vo. Paper. Price, 60 cents, *net.*

Outlines of Economic Theory.

By HERBERT JOSEPH DAVENPORT. 8vo. $2.00, *net.*

The book is in two parts, of which the first sets forth the theory of economic science, but following the usual discussion of wealth, value, production, wages, profits, rent, population, capital and interest, distribution, combination and monopolies, trades-unions, taxation, currency, bimetallism, international trade and currency, commercial crises, the tariff, etc. ; a second part is introduced entitled Economics in Art. Its discussions are of great practical value and are timely, touching on the competitive system, coöperation and profit-sharing, state and municipal ownership, taxation, the eight-hour day, the apprentice system, sweating shops, the labour of women and children, the unemployed, the currency, free coinage of silver, etc., etc.

An Introduction to Public Finance.

By Prof. CARL C. PLEHN (Univ. of Cal.) 12mo. $1.60, *net.*

An elementary text-book offering a simple outline of those things which are necessary to prepare the student for independent research ; a brief discussion of the leading principles that are generally accepted ; a statement of the unsettled principles, with the grounds of controversy ; and sufficient references to enable the student to form some opinion for himself.

THE MACMILLAN COMPANY,

NEW YORK.   CHICAGO   SAN FRANCISCO.

Valuable Collateral Reading

IN

ECONOMICS, HISTORY, ETC.

By JAMES BRYCE, M.P., D.C.L.

The American Commonwealth for Students' Use.

Revised by Mr. BRYCE, with the Assistance of Prof. JESSE MACY, of Iowa College. This is not a mere condensation of the larger work, but a restatement, briefer and in a form more carefully adapted to use as a text-book, of the valuable material in Mr. Bryce's "American Commonwealth," a knowledge of which is conceded to be indispensable to any one who would acquire a just estimate of American institutions.

"It is a genuine pleasure to commend to our readers the abridged edition of 'The American Commonwealth' just issued by The Macmillan Company. Mr. Bryce's book, which has heretofore been issued only in two volumes, has no peer as a commentary upon American political institutions."—*Public Opinion.*

"Mr. Bryce's work is the best book yet published on the form, operation and character of American institutions. This edition is abridged especially for class room work in colleges and high schools. It is not merely a curtailment of the larger work, but it is a concentration of it and in some respects has new matter bringing it down to date. No European writer, not excepting De Tocqueville, ever studied the workings of American institutions with such success as has Professor Bryce. He has accomplished what is impossible to most Englishmen ; namely, kept his British prejudice out of the discussion of American institutions."—*Gunton's Magazine.*

The American Commonwealth.

2 vols. Large 12 mo. Third edition. Revised throughout. Price $3.50, *net.*

"His work rises at once to an eminent place among studies of great nations and their institutions. It is, so far as America goes, a work unique in scope, spirit and knowledge. There is nothing like it anywhere extant—nothing that approaches it. . . Without exaggeration, it may be called the most considerable and gratifying tribute that has yet been bestowed upon us by an Englishman, and perhaps by even England herself. . . One despairs in an attempt to give in a single newspaper article an adequate account of a work so infused with knowledge and sparkling with suggestion . . Every thoughtful American will read it, and will long hold in grateful remembrance its author's name."—*New York Times.*

"Mr. Bryce's study of the American commonwealth stands alone, both by reason of its scope and of the rare acumen and fairness which distinguish it. The book is one which should never be suffered to go out of print, and which every American, young and old, should read and deeply ponder."—*New Orleans Times Democrat.*

"The work is an unbiased and high-minded critical opinion of the main features of American institutions by a man of erudition and culture, and latterly with a wide and srccessful experience in practical political affairs, and it is a good sign of the tendency of modern American opinion that his book is so widely read and circulated in the United States. It is one which no thoughtful American should leave unread."—*The Open Court.*

THE MACMILLAN COMPANY,

NEW YORK.   CHICAGO.   SAN FRANCISCO.

THE CITIZEN,

PUBLISHED MONTHLY,

By the American Society for the Extension of University Teaching.

The *JUNE* number **Contains** the following :

Annual Subscription, $1.00. Single Copy, 10 cts.

Address communications to

THE EDITOR,

111 South 15th Street, Philadelphia.

JOHNS HOPKINS UNIVERSITY
Studies in History and Politics.

Edited by Herbert B. Adams.

Fifteenth Series, 1897.   Subscription, $3.00.

AMERICAN ECONOMIC HISTORY.

I-II. THE TOBACCO INDUSTRY IN VIRGINIA SINCE 1860. By B. W. Arnold.
    Paper 50 cents.
III-IV-V. THE STREET RAILWAY SYSTEM [OF PHILADELPHIA. By F. W.
    Speirs. Paper 75 cents; cloth $1.00.
THE FINANCIAL HISTORY OF BALTIMORE. By J. H. Hollander.
THE AMERICAN SCHOOL OF POLITICAL ECONOMY. By Sidney Sherwood.
HISTORY AND THEORY OF TRUSTS. By H. L. Moore.
STATE BANKING IN MARYLAND. By A. C. Bryan.
STATE TAX COMMISSIONS IN THE UNITED STATES. By J. W. Chapman.
THE ECONOMIC HISTORY OF THE BALTIMORE & OHIO RAILROAD (1827-53). By
    Milton Reizenstein.
THE SOUTH AMERICAN TRADE OF BALTIMORE. By F. R. Rutter.
IRRIGATION IN UTAH. By C. H. Brough.

Other papers will be from time to time announced.

ANNUAL SERIES, 1883-1896.

SERIES I.—Local Institutions. 479 pages. $4.00.
SERIES II.—Institutions and Economics. 629 pages. $4.00.
SERIES III.—Maryland, Virginia and Washington. 595 pages. $4.00.
SERIES IV.—Municip l Government and Land Tenure. 600 pages. $3.50.
SERIES V.—Municip Government, History and Politics. 559 pages. $3.50.
SERIES VI.—The History of Co-operation in the United States. 540 pages. $3.50.
SERIES VII.—Social Science, Municipal and Federal Government. $3.50.
SERIES VIII.—History, Politics and Education. 625 pages. 8vo. $3.50.
SERIES IX.—Education, History and Politics. 640 pages. 8vo. $3.50.
SERIES X.—Church and State: Columbus and America. 630 pages. 8vo. $3.50.
SERIES XI.—Labor, Slavery and Self-Government. 574 pages. 8vo. $3.50.
SERIES XII.—Institutional and Economic History. 626 pages. 8vo. $3.50.
SERIES XIII.—South Carolina, Maryland and Virginia. 606 pages. 8vo. $3.50.
SERIES XIV.—Baltimore, Slavery, and Constitutional History. 592 pages. 8vo. $3.50.

RECENT EXTRA VOLUMES.

THE SUPREME COURT OF THE UNITED STATES. By W. W. Willoughby. 124
    pp. 8vo. cloth. $1.15.
THE INTERCOURSE BETWEEN JAPAN AND THE UNITED STATES. Inazo
    (Ota) Nitobe. 198 pp. 8vo. cloth. $1.25.
SPANISH INSTITUTIONS OF THE SOUTHWEST. By Frank W. Blackmar. 380
    pp. and 31 plates. 8vo. cloth. $2.00.
INTRODUCTION TO THE STUDY OF THE CONSTITUTION. By M. M. Cohn.
    250 pp. 8vo. cloth. $1.50.
THE OLD ENGLISH MANOR. By C. M. Andrews. 280 pp. 8vo. cloth. $1.50.
AMERICA: ITS GEOGRAPHICAL HISTORY, 1492-1892. By W. B. Scaife.   6
    8vo. cloth. $1.50.
FLORENTINE LIFE DURING THE RENAISSANCE. By W. B. Sc fe. 256 pp. 8vo.
    cloth. $1.50.
THE SOUTHERN QUAKERS AND SLAVERY. By Stephen B. Wi ks. 414 pp. 8vo.
    Cloth. $2.00.
THE FRENCH REVOLUTION AS SEEN BY AMERICANS OF THE EIGHTEENTH
    CENTURY. (In press.)

The set of fourteen series is now offered uniformly bound in cloth, for $42.00, and in-
cluding subscription to the current (fifteenth) series, $45.00. The fourteen series with
fourteen extra volumes, altogether twenty-eight volumes, in cloth, for $60.00.
    Orders should be addressed to
                    THE JOHNS HOPKINS PRESS, BALTIMORE, MARYLAND.

Librairie Guillaumin et Cie., Rue Richelieu 14, à PARIS.

Journal des Economistes

REVUE MENSUELLE

De la Science économique et de la Statistique

CINQUANTE SIXIÈME ANNÉE.

Rédacteur en chef : G. DE MOLINARI,

Correspondant de l'Institut.

Conditions de l'abonnement :

France un an, **36** fr.
Union postale, **38** fr.
Un numéro, **3** fr. **50**.

Revue Politique et Parlementaire

RÉDACTION RUE DE L'UNIVERSITÉ, 110.

Directeur : Marcel FOURNIER.

SOMMAIRE DU N° DE MAI 1897.

Abonnement Annuel: France : 25 fr.; Colonies et Union Postale : 30 fr. ; le N° : 3 fr.

Les abonnements partent de Janvier ou de Juillet.

A. COLIN et Cie, Editeurs, 5, RUE DE MÉZIÈRES, PARIS.

Giornale Degli Economisti

RIVISTA MENSILE DEGLI INTERESSI ITALIANI

Sommario del Fascicolo del Maggio, 1897

ROMA.

PRESSO LA DIREZIONE,

Monte Savello, Palazzo Orsini.

Prezzo del fascicols lire 3.

A Quarterly Review of Religion, Ethics and Theology.

(200 pp., 8vo. : issued the first of March, June, September and December.)

"There is always something good to read, because there is always earnest thinking in the NEW WORLD which is the quarterly organ of "reverent breadth" in American religious thought. . . . . Altogether the NEW WORLD is a periodical which deserves much attention. There is hardly its equivalent on this side of the Atlantic."

The *Spectator* (London).

Contents of No. XX, December, 1896.

Contents of No. XXI, March, 1897.

Contents of No. XXII, June, 1897.

Single Number, 75 cts.; 3s. Yearly Subscription, $3.00 ; 12s.

BOSTON AND NEW YORK:

HOUGHTON, MIFFLIN & CO., Publishers.

LONDON: GAY & BIRD, Bedford St.

1897   SIXTY-SEVENTH YEAR

THE

BIBLIOTHECA SACRA

A Religious and Sociological Quarterly

CONDUCTED BY

G. FREDERICK WRIGHT   Z. SWIFT HOLBROOK

OBERLIN, O.   CHICAGO, ILL.

ASSOCIATED WITH : EDWARDS A. PARK, FRANK H. FOSTER, JUDSON SMITH, D.
W. SIMON, WM. M. BARBOUR, SAMUEL IVES CURTISS, CHAS. F. THWING,
A. A. BERLE, W. E. BARTON, E. H. JOHNSON, JACOB COOPER,
AND E. W. BEMIS.

CONTENTS OF THE JANUARY NUMBER.

CONTENTS OF THE APRIL NUMBER.

CONTENTS OF THE JULY NUMBER.

The *Sociological, Critical,* and *Semitic Notes* and the *Book Reviews* form an important feature of the numbers.

Single Number, **75 cents.** Yearly Subscription, **$3.00.** For Special Terms for 1897 to New Subscribers and sample pages,

Address   **BIBLIOTHECA SACRA CO., Oberlin, Ohio, U. S. A**

RECENT PUBLICATIONS ON

Political, Social and Economic Topics.

A sketch of the American Academy of Political and Social Science, containing a record of its progress since 1889, a copy of its Charter and Constitution, and a list of its officers and council will be sent on application.

AMERICAN ACADEMY OF POLITICAL AND SOCIAL SCIENCE,

STATION B, PHILADELPHIA, U. S. A.

MUNICIPAL AFFAIRS.

A Quarterly Magazine Devoted to the Consideration of City Problems from the Standpoint of the Tax-payer and Citizen.

Among the subjects to which attention will be given in the pages of *Municipal Affairs* are the following:

Baths and Lavatories,	Charities,	Excise,
Finance,	Hospitals,	Libraries,
Assessments for Benefit,	Prisons,	Museums,
Franchises,	Docks,	Sewage Disposal,
Transportation,	Protection against Fire,	Amusements,
Public Works,	Street Cleaning,	Public Art (including
Gas and Water Supply,	Police,	Music, Paintings,Statuary, Monuments,etc)
Electric Lighting,	Parks,	
Schools,	Markets,	

VOL. 1, NO. 1, MARCH, 1897.

A BIBLIOGRAPHY OF MUNICIPAL ADMINISTRATION AND CITY CONDITIONS. By ROBERT C. BROOKS. Published in full in the March number of *Municipal Affairs*, Vol. I, No. 1; paper, 12mo., 224 pp. 50 cents.

—A municipal biography that is by far the most complete, so far as we are aware, that anyone has ever compiled.—*Review of Reviews.*

—The bibliography will be invaluable to all reformers, public officials and students of civics.—*Independent, New York.*

—Indispensable to clubs, committees, and individuals who undertake investigations or the preparation of reports or bills.—*Times, New York.*

—The publication is a most valuable one and is just what is needed. One can find with the utmost facility the entire attainable literature bearing upon any question or feature of city administration.—*City and State, Philadelphia.*

—The bibliography is by far the most complete that has been published, containing all references of importance, not merely to municipal administration but also to general municipal problems.—*Annals of the American Academy.*

VOL. 1, NO. 2, JUNE, 1897. (Now ready.)

Why New York should Own Its Gas Supply, A Controversy. By Hon. Edward M. Grout and Allen Ripley Foote.

Municipal Reform during the Past Year. By Clinton Rogers Woodruff.

The Finances of New York City. By Henry DeForest Baldwin.

American Political Ideas and Institutions in their Relation to the Conditions of City Life. By Dr. Leo S. Rowe.

Book Reviews, Digests of Periodical Literature, Biliographical Index, etc.

Subscription Price $1.00 per Year. Single Numbers 25c. each.

(Except Vol. I, No. 1, containing Bibliography—price of which is 50 cts.)

Address all communications to

Committee on Municipal Administration,

52 William Street, New York City.

International Journal of Ethics.

A Quarterly (now in its seventh year) devoted to individual and social ethics. England, France, Austria, Italy Denmark, and the United States are represented on the
editorial committee. Each nnmber contains articles, discussions and reviews by prominent ethical writers in different countries.

Among the articles which have recently appeared are the following :

THE ETHICS OF RELIGIOUS CONFORMITY. HENRY SIDGWICK.

THE MORAL ASPECTS OF SOCIALISM. SIDNEY BALL.

THE ETHICAL LIFE AND CONCEPTIONS OF THE JAPANESE. TOKIWO YOKOI.

IS PLEASURE THE SUMMUM BONUM? JAMES SETH.

THE ETHICAL ASPECTS OF SOCIAL SCIENCE. LESTER F. WARD.

RIGHTS AND DUTIES. J. S. MACKENZIE.

THE JEWISH QUESTION IN ITS RECENT ASPECTS. MORRIS JASTROW, JR.

INTERNATIONAL ARBITRATION. JOHN WESTLAKE.

IS THE FAMILY DECLINING? J. H. MUIRHEAD.

THE MORAL TEACHINGS OF THE ANCIENT ZOROASTRIAN RELIGION. A. V.
WILLIAMS JACKSON.

PROFESSOR SIDGWICK ON THE ETHICS OF RELIGIOUS CONFORMITY. Rev.
HASTINGS RASHDALL, Hertford College, Oxford.

THE ETHICAL AND POLITICAL PROBLEMS OF NEW JAPAN. TOKIWO YOKIO,
Tokyo, Japan.

MORALITY AND THE BELIEF IN THE SUPERNATURAL. Prof. ELIZA RITCHIE,
Wellesley, College.

THE RESTORATION OF ECONOMICS TO ETHICS. CHARLES S. DEVAS, Royal Uni
versity of Ireland.

THE RESPONSIBILITIES OF THE LAWYER. JOSEPH B. WARNER, Boston.

THE PSYCHOLOGY OF SOCIAL PROGRESS. HELEN BOSANQUET, London.

THE MORAL LIFE OF THE EARLY ROMANS. FRANK GRANGER, University College, Nottingham.

SOCIAL LIFE AND MORALITY IN INDIA. MUHAMMAD ABDUL GHANI, India.

The July number will contain articles on " *The Ethical Side of the Free Silver Cam-
paign*," by F. J. Stimson, Esq., of Boston, and " *The Treatment of Prisoners*," by Rev.
William Douglas Morrison, of London.

Considerable space is devoted in each number to Discussions and Book Reviews.

Philadelphia: INTERNATIONAL JOURNAL OF ETHICS, 1305 Arch Street.

Yearly, $2.50. Single Numbers, 65 cts.

The Quarterly Journal of Economics.

Published for Harvard University.

Books, periodicals, and manuscript to be addressed, EDITORS of QUARTERLY JOURNAL OF ECONOMICS, Cambridge, Mass.

Business letters, etc., to be addressed, GEORGE H. ELLIS, Publisher, 141 Franklin Street, Boston, Mass.

Editor.

F. W. TAUSSIG.

Associate Editors.

C. F. DUNBAR.   W. J. ASHLEY.

EDWARD CUMMINGS.

Among the other writers in recent volumes have been :

CONTENTS FOR JANUARY, 1897.

CONTENTS FOR APRIL, 1897.

Studies in History, Economics and Public Law,

— EDITED BY —

THE FACULTY OF POLITICAL SCIENCE

OF COLUMBIA UNIVERSITY.

RECENT NUMBERS.

VOLUME VI.—601 pp.

HISTORY OF PROPRIETARY GOVERNMENT IN PENNSYLVANIA. By William Robert Shepherd, Ph.D.—Price, $4.00 ; bound, $4.50.

VOLUME VII.—512 pp.

1. HISTORY OF THE TRANSITION FROM PROVINCIAL TO COMMONWEALTH GOVERNMENT IN MASSACHUSETTS. By Harry A. Cushing, Ph.D. Price, $2.00.

2. SPECULATION ON THE STOCK AND PRODUCE EXCHANGES OF THE UNITED STATES. By Henry Crosby Emery, Ph.D. Price, $1.50.

VOLUME VIII.

1. THE STRUGGLE BETWEEN PRESIDENT JOHNSON AND CONGRESS OVER RECONSTRUCTION. By Charles Ernest Chadsey, Ph.D. Price, $1.00.

2. RECENT CENTRALIZING TENDENCIES IN STATE EDUCATIONAL ADMINISTRATION. By William Clarence Webster, A.M. Price, 75 cts.

3. THE ABOLITION OF PRIVATEERING AND THE DECLARATION OF PARIS. By Francis R. Stark, LL.B., Ph.D. Price $1.00.

4. (To appear shortly.)

VOLUME IX.

1. ENGLISH LOCAL GOVERNMENT OF TO-DAY. A Study of the Relations of Central and Local Governments. By Milo Roy Maltbie, Ph.D. Price, $2.00.

VOLUMES I to VII (except Vol. VI), Price, for each Volume, $3.00 ; bound, $3.50.

For further particulars apply to

PROF. EDWIN R. A. SELIGMAN, Columbia University, or to THE MACMILLAN COMPANY, New York.

MONOGRAPHS.

VOLUME I.

No. 1. Report of the Organization of the American Economic Association. By Richard T. Ely, Ph.D., Secretary. *Price 50 cents.*

Nos. 2 and 3. The Relation of the Modern Municipality to the Gas Supply. By Edmund J. James, Ph.D. *Price 75 cents.*

No. 4. Co-operation in a Western City. By Albert Shaw, Ph.D. *Price 75 cents.*

No. 5. Co-operation in New England. By Edward W. Bemis, Ph.D. *Price 75 cents.*

No. 6. Relation of the State to Industrial Action. By Henry C. Adams, Ph.D. *Price 75 cents.*

VOLUME II.

No. 1. Three Phases of Co-operation in the West. By Amos G. Warner, Ph.D. *Price 75 cents.*

No. 2. Historical Sketch of the Finances of Pennsylvania. By T. K. Worthington, Ph.D. *Price 75 cents.*

No. 3. The Railway Question. By Edmund J. James, Ph.D. *Price 75 cents.*

No. 4. The Early History of the English Woolen Industry. By W. J. Ashley M.A. *Price 75 cents.*

No. 5. Two Chapters on the Mediæval Guilds of England. By Edwin R. A. Seligman, Ph.D. *Price 75 cents.*

No. 6. The Relation of Modern Municipalities to Quasi-Public Works. By H. C. Adams, George W. Knight, Davis R. Dewey, Charles Moore, Frank J. Goodnow and Arthur Yager. *Price 75 cents.*

VOLUME III.

No. 1. Three Papers Read at Meeting in Boston: "Statistics in Colleges," by Carroll D. Wright; "Sociology and Political Economy," by F. H. Giddings; "The Legal-Tender Decisions," by E. J. James. *Price 75 cents.*

No. 2. Capital and its Earnings. By John B. Clark, A.M. *Price 75 cents.*

No. 3 consists of three parts: "The Manual Laboring Class," by General F. A. Walker; "Mine Labor in the Hocking Valley," by E. W. Bemis, Ph.D.; "Report of the Second Annual Meeting," by Richard T. Ely, Secretary. *Price 75 cents.*

Nos. 4 and 5. Statistics and Economics. By Richmond Mayo-Smith, A.M. *Price $1.00.*

No. 6. The Stability of Prices. By Simon N. Patten, Ph.D. *Price 75 cents.*

PUBLICATIONS OF THE AMERICAN ECONOMIC ASSOCIATION

VOLUME IV.

No. 1. Contributions to the Wages Question: "The Theory of Wages," by Stuart Wood, Ph.D.; "Possibility of a Scientific Law of Wages," by John B. Clark, A.M. *Price 75 cents.*

No. 2. Socialism in England. By Sidney Webb, LL.B. *Price 75 cents.*

No. 3. Road Legislation for the American State. By Jeremiah W. Jenks, Ph.D. *Price 75 cents.*

No. 4. Report of the Proceedings of Third Annual Meeting of the American Economic Association, by Richard T. Ely, Secretary; with addresses by Dr. William Pepper and Gen. F. A. Walker. *Price 75 cents.*

No. 5. Three Papers Read at Third Annual Meeting: "Malthus and Ricardo," by S. N. Patten; "The Study of Statistics," by D. R. Dewey, and "Analysis in Political Economy," by W. W. Folwell. *Price 75 cents.*

No. 6. An Honest Dollar. By President E. Benjamin Andrews. *Price 75 cents.*

VOLUME V.

No. 1. The Industrial Transition in Japan. By Yeijiro Ono, Ph.D. *Price $1.00.*

No. 2. Two Prize Essays on Child-Labor: I. By William F. Willoughby, Ph.D.; II. By Miss Clare de Graffenried. *Price 75 cents.*

Nos. 3 and 4. Two Papers on the Canal Question. I. By Edmund J. James, Ph.D.; II. By Lewis M. Haupt, A.M., C.E. *Price $1.00.*

No. 5. History of the New York Property Tax. By John Christopher Schwab, A.M., Ph.D. *Price $1.00.*

No. 6. The Educational Value of Political Economy. By Simon N. Patten, Ph.D. *Price 75 cents.*

VOLUME VI.

No. 1 and 2. Report of the Proceedings of the Fourth Annual Meeting of the American Economic Association. *Price $1.00.*

No. 3. I. Government Forestry Abroad. By Gifford Pinchot. II. The Present Condition of the Forests on the Public Lands. By Edward A. Bowers. III. Practicability of an American Forest Administration. By B. E. Fernow. *Price 75 cents.*

Nos. 4 and 5. Municipal Ownership of Gas in the United States. By Edward W. Bemis, Ph.D. *Price $1.00.*

No. 6. State Railroad Commissions and How they May be Made Effective. By Frederick C. Clark, Ph.D. *Price 75 cents.*

PUBLICATIONS OF THE AMERICAN ECONOMIC ASSOCIATION.

VOLUME VII.

No. 1. The Silver Situation in the United States. By F. W. Taussig, LL.B., Ph.D. *Price 75 cents.*

Nos. 2 and 3. On the Shifting and Incidence of Taxation. By Edwin R. A. Seligman, Ph.D. *Price $1.00.*

Nos. 4 and 5. Sinking Funds. By Edward A. Ross, Ph.D. *Price $1.00.*

No. 6. The Reciprocity Treaty with Canada of 1854. By F. E. Haynes, Ph.D. *Price 75 cents.*

VOLUME VIII.

No. 1. Report of the Proceedings of the Fifth Annual Meeting of the American Economic Association. *Price 75 cents.*

Nos. 2 and 3. The Housing of the Poor in American Cities. By Marcus T. Reynolds, Ph.B., M.A. *Price $1.00.*

Nos. 4 and 5. Public Assistance of the Poor in France. By Emily Greene Balch, A.B. *Price $1.00.*

No. 6. The First Stages of the Tariff Policy of the United States. By William Hill, A.M. *Price $1.00.*

VOLUME IX.

Hand-Book and Report of the Sixth Annual Meeting. *Price 50 cents.*

Nos. 1 and 2. Progressive Taxation in Theory and Practice. By Edwin R. A. Seligman, Ph.D. *Price $1.00, cloth $1.50.*

No. 3. The Theory of Transportation. By Charles H. Cooley. *Price 75 cents.*

No. 4. Sir William Petty: A Study in English Economic Literature. By Wilson Lloyd Bevan, M.A., Ph.D. *Price 75 cents.*

Nos. 5 and 6. Papers Read at the Seventh Annual Meeting: "The Modern Appeal to Legal Forces in Economic Life," (President's annual address), by John B. Clark, Ph.D. ; "The Chicago Strike," by Carroll D. Wright, LL.D. ; "The Unemployed," by Davis R. Dewey, Ph.D. ; "Population and Capital," by Arthur T. Hadley, M.A. ; "The Pope and the Encyclical on Labor," by John Graham Brooks. *Price $1.00.*

VOLUME X.

Hand-Book and Report of the Seventh Annual Meeting. *Price 50 cents.*

Nos. 1, 2 and 3. The Canadian Banking System, 1817-1890. By R. M. Breckenridge, Ph.D. *Price $1.50; cloth $2.50.*

No. 4. Poor Laws of Massachusetts and New York. By John Cummings, Ph.D. *Price 75 cents.*

Nos. 5 and 6. Letters of Ricardo to McCulloch, 1816-1823. Edited, with introduction and annotations by J. H. Hollander, Ph.D. *Price $1.25; cloth $2.00.*

PUBLICATIONS OF THE AMERICAN ECONOMIC ASSOCIATION.

VOLUME XI.

Nos. 1, 2 and 3.   Race Traits and Tendencies of the American Negro.   By F. L.
Hoffman, F.S.S.   *Price $1.25; cloth $2.00.*
No. 4.   Appreciation and Interest.   By Irving Fisher, Ph.D.   *Price 75 cents.*

TO APPEAR SOON.

The Cotton Industry: An Essay in American Economic History.   By M. B.
Hammond.

ECONOMIC STUDIES.

VOLUME I.

Hand-Book and Report of the Eighth Annual Meeting.   *Price 50 cents.*
No. 1.   The Theory of Economic Progress, by John B. Clark, Ph.D.   The Re-
lation of Changes in the Volume of the Currency to Prosperity, by
Francis A. Walker, LL.D.   *Price 50 cents.*
No. 2.   The Adjustment of Wages to Efficiency.   Three papers : Gain Sharing,
by H. R. Towne ; The Premium Plan, by F. A. Halsey ; A Piece-Rate
System, by F. W. Taylor.   *Price 50 cents.*
No. 3.   The Populist Movement.   By Frank L. McVey, Ph.D.   *Price 50 cents.*
No. 4.   The Present Monetary Situation.   By Professor W. Lexis.   Translated by,
John Cummings, Ph.D.   *Price 50 cents.*
Nos. 5-6.   The Street Railway Problem in Cleveland.   By William Rowland
Hopkins.   *Price 75 cents.*

VOLUME II.

Hand-Book and Report of the Ninth Annual Meeting.   *Price 50 cents.*
No. 1.   Economics and Jurisprudence.   By Henry C. Adams, Ph.D.   *Price 50 cts.*
No. 2.   The Saloon Question in Chicago.   By John E. George, Ph.B.   *Price 50 cts.*
No. 3.   The General Property Tax in California.   By Carl C. Plehn, Ph.D.   *Price
50 cents.*
No. 4.   Area and Population of the United States at the Eleventh Census.   By
Walter F. Willcox, Ph.D.   *Price 50 cents.*

*The Studies are issued bi-monthly.   The Monographs are issued at irregular
intervals in the discretion of the publication committee.*
*Price of the several volumes of Monographs, unbound, $4.00 each.   Bound in
cloth, $5.00 each for single volumes, $4.00 for each additional volume.   The set of
ten bound volumes, $41.00, sent prepaid.   Any bound volume will be sent post-paid
to members for 75 cents in exchange for the unbound numbers, if returned prepaid
in good condition.   Copies can also be furnished in half morocco at 50 cents per
volume additional to the price in cloth.*
*Separate subscriptions by non-members, libraries, etc., for the Studies, $2.50 per
year ; or $4.00 for all the publications.   Any single monograph may be obtained
at the price given in the list.*
One-sixth Discount to Members and Subscribers on all Orders.

Address applications for membership and in-
quiries to the

SECRETARY *of the* AMERICAN
ECONOMIC ASSOCIATION.
Ithaca, N. Y.

Address Subscriptions and orders for
Studies and Monographs to the publishers,

THE MACMILLAN CO.,
66 Fifth Avenue,   -   -   *New York.*

www.ingramcontent.com/pod-product-compliance
Lightning Source LLC
Chambersburg PA
CBHW031453270326
41930CB00007B/981